A journey through a psychotic breakdown

Douglas Gonçalves

EXPERIENCE IS NOT WHAT
HAPPENS TO YOU.

IT IS WHAT YOU DO WITH
WHAT HAPPENS TO YOU.

ALDOUS HUXLEY

Table of Contents

Preface 6

Keywords 9

The meeting (4 April 2004)................................12

O Surto...16

11 September 2001 29

Childhood and ancestry....................................38

Hospitalisation...44

Medicines and Healing 55

Conclusions..73

Testimonies...76

Acknowledgements..101

About the Author...103

Who we are 105

Preface

Because of my work as a chaplain in a cancer hospital, I accompany people daily as they experience the final moments of their lives. My role in these situations is to identify possible sources of spiritual suffering that prevent the patient or their family members from experiencing a certain amount of peace amid the sadness that comes from anticipatory grief.

The question 'Are you at peace?' is an opportunity to identify this suffering, usually confirmed by a negative answer to the question. The belief that life was lived without the intended meaning we wanted to give it and that a lot of time was wasted without enough attention given to the most significant relationships, almost always with family and friends, is among the most common causes of suffering at the end of life.

Here we are inserted into the universe of spirituality, which in the world of health has been consensually defined as 'that aspect of humanity that concerns how individuals seek and express sense and meaning, and how they connect with themselves, with others, nature, the moment and the sacred or meaningful.'

As the great spiritual traditions recognise, especially in their more mystical lines, the contemplation of finitude and death reveals itself as one of the central means by which the individual becomes capable of distinguishing more easily between what is essential and what is not essential in life. 'Teach us to number our days so that we may attain a wise heart', sings the psalmist in the Judeo-Christian Scriptures, echoing the story of Prince Siddhartha Gautama, who becomes the Enlightened One (Buddha) only after departing from the royal palace to the encounter with the realities of illness, old age, and death.

Paradoxically, contemplating death can lead us to experience a fuller life. In contrast, the experience of illness can contribute to our health by making us re-examine our lifestyle, choices, and priorities, regardless of the social and cultural resistance we beat to obey the prevailing standards.

To accept that being well adapted to a sick society is not a sign of health, as the Indian philosopher Jiddu Krishnamurti reminds us, leads us to question who among us can actually be considered healthy or sick. Therefore, the search for an answer to this question can only do with the contribution of disciplines other than medicine: among them, sociology, psychology, anthropology, philosophy, theology, arts, and literature.

In our effort to understand the human being, the study of DNA is not enough, as the British psychiatrist and writer Theodore Dalrymple says: reading Shakespeare is also fundamental. And it is precisely the brilliant English poet who warns us, in the dialogue between Macbeth and the doctor of his madly stricken wife, that there is no single technical or scientific solution capable of making our pain disappear and quieting our most profound spiritual yearnings.

'Canst thou not minister to a mind diseased

Pluck from the memory a rooted sorrow,

Raze out the written troubles of the brain,

And with some sweet oblivious antidote,

Cleanse the stuff'd bosom of that perilous stuff

Which weighs upon the heart?'

The doctor responds concisely:

'Therin the patient

Must minister to himself.'

'A journey through a psychotic breakdown', written by Douglas, is a vivid account of his anguish, pain and memories, and a map of the authorial path he had drawn and trodden in his search for himself. The author celebrates the success of his medical treatment and the (re)encounter with himself, a primordial task of spirituality, singing the song 'Epitaph' by Titãs. The symbolism of this choice says much about the moving story portrayed in this book: the death and rebirth of a man.

Dr Roberto Pereira Miguel

Chaplain at Moffitt Cancer Center – Tampa, FL/USA

Theologian (Universidade Presbiteriana Mackenzie - São Paulo), Master in Religious Sciences (Pontifícia Universidade Católica - São Paulo) and Doctor in Collective Health (UNIFESP - São Paulo)

Keywords

NEEDINESS

CONTROLS

SELFISHNESS

AUDITS

EXCESS

SELF-LOVE

ACCOUNTS PAYABLE

LONELINESS

DEMANDS

KINDNESS

BEAUTY

RESIGNATIONS

GOALS

BREAKUP

PASSIONS

CONSTANT SEARCH

STRESS

ANXIETY

FEES.

His mind is overloaded, and he will have a nervous breakdown; he seeks help from his family, but he lives in another town. He is alone.

How it all started

Everything started during the last management meeting when he showed some unusual behaviour. His colleagues noticed something different; however, it went without much fanfare, except for some mental disorder that was not perceived back then.

The meeting
(4 April 2004)

This time, our regular meeting was in Santo An•ré, a town near São Paulo, with •irectors an• managers from the economic bran•s. There were 40 people altogether, belonging to various •epartments. We ha• members of the DC (Direction Committee) who are corporate lea•ers in the areas of Marketing, Human Resources, Foo• an• Beverage, Maintenance, an• other managers from all over the country. It was a melting pot of accents an• cultures from all over Brazil an• overseas, resulting in an enriching synergy of behaviour, custom, an• experience.

During four long •ays, I behave• myself an• controlle• my primal instincts superbly. That meant keeping in check my •etermination to lea• an• resolve everything simultaneously, an• that went without mentioning, my chronic anxiety an• lack of patience.

Hol• on tight, man!

I was surprise• with my self-control, so much so that I contacte• one of the meeting coor•inators to report my feeling of •iscomfort regar•ing irrelevant interventions by some people. I also approache• a colleague •ebuting in a corporate position an• was working on his presentation about his achievements an• new challenges.

It was har• to finish. Hormones were pulsing in a super competitive environment.

On this occasion, I coul• meet the latest managers to exchange experiences. The bran• is rising, an• a new member joins the group •aily.

By the end of next year, there will be 53 hotels in the economic brands. Our group consists of young and enthusiastic managers. Among them, a considerable number of 'jokers' came from the hospitality sector of the group itself or the market – my case.

To unwind from the stressful routine, we have a two-team contest that aims to play tricks on the opponent members. Both teams are well-organised, with a mission and vision statement, including a baptism ceremony for new comrades. The idea is the same for both teams: making minor mischief to rival members and those not yet affiliated, or rather, without political inclination, and convincing the latter to join one's team. The two teams are The Evil Gang, also known as EG, and The Good Gang, also called GG, to which I belong.

The Evil Gang was founded over a year ago and has a standard vertical organisation chart with some exciting actions. One of them was nominating the director of the economic brand as 'The Evil Trainee' during the yearly meeting of the whole group at the Costa do Sauípe in Bahia[1], including a baptism ceremony and an exclusive t-shirt.

On the other hand, the Good Gang, although also pranksters themselves, have a kindness planner, namely me. Despite being younger than its rival, GG has already done some good deeds. For example, they once stole t-shirts from members of EG, including The Evil Trainee's, and donated them to beggars in the Praça da Sé[2] in São Paulo.

GG's organisation chart is horizontal, contrary to EG's vertical one. It means we do not have such a thing as a retrograde despot, also known as a president, who can decide the future and, often in his way, restrict his fellow members' will. Therefore, I believe such a corporate structure is much more advantageous, inclusive and democratic.

1. TN – Costa do Sauípe is a very well-known all-inclusive resort on the coast of Bahia state in Brazil.
2. TN – Praça da Sé, the See Square, is a public space in the heart of São Paulo

During the last meeting, this team presented a photograph show-ing the Santo André manager, an EG member, in which he dressed as Pebbles Flintstone. It was our way to show appreciation for the great welcome provided by the local team. There was also a show by a famous quick-change artist, during which we celebrated the wedding of 'Little Feet', Santo André's supervisor. There is a rumour that he got this nick-name because he failed the blood spot test when he was born[3].

Jokes aside, the Director-General of the whole group's brands paid us a visit on the last day of the meeting. During the chat, we were able to align our strategic guidelines. We also learnt more details about our actions along with the Hotel Association; furthermore, he informed us that there had been talks with public bodies to reduce a specific federal tax, which would greatly benefit our trade.

I remember that I paid attention to the position of the Direc-tor-General's chair and mine. They were both the furthest from the table, in perfect alignment. Then, I had an insight: we were similar in some way, and I would be his natural successor, endowed with a lead-er's personality.

I then had the opportunity to describe to everyone the recent ar-ticle mentioning the actual value of our products. I explained that the customers' reasonable expectations change with time: yesterday's re-finement has become today's norm. For example, I mentioned salmon and dry tomato, food items appreciated by everyone but only widely enjoyed by some part of the population, and so still restricted to the luxury segment. I also emphasised that the three most important values were: Time, Space and Silence.

In my speech, I also stressed the importance of having a certified economic product. When asked who my customers were, I included

3. TN – The blood spot test is a newborn screening test that takes a blood sample from the baby's heel to check for nine rare but serious conditions (Source: NHS/ UK)

competitors and those mentioned by my colleagues. Our company has brands in all industry segments, from economic to luxury, with lesser or greater value-added benefits. Consequently, competitors, in turn, are our guests.

Following this explanation, I stated why I was in the economic hub, given that I had already worked in a hotel whose average daily rate was the highest in Latin America. I said I was not crazy and that I was learning a great deal at a company that is socially committed to the continuous improvement of its processes and the well-being of its employees and the community.

In conclusion, I commended the company for its significant steps forward and for becoming increasingly involved in social actions and environmental preservation. I concluded my speech by stating my pride in being part of the team. A genuine feeling of belonging. Wow!

At this point, everyone rose to their feet in applause.

HAVE I LOST IT???

THE PSYCHOTIC BREAKDOWN

O Surto

The Psychotic Breakdown 29 April 2004 – late afternoon/evening

He went to his bedroom, anxious to pack and return to São Paulo, but the first setback came: the safe did not open. He typed the code again to no avail and a third time with the same result. Finally, calling reception, he informed the situation and asked for his friends in the lobby, who would get a ride with him. Unfortunately, they would have to wait while a service technician opened the safe and he could get his belongings. It did not take long for a kind girl to come and try to solve the problem, but she was unsuccessful. While waiting for another service person, he packed his suitcase, sat on the bed, turned on the air conditioner and TV, and waited for help. As a diligent hotelier, he paid attention to all the room's details and memorised the address, the telephone and the safe serial numbers. It certainly was the beginning of the BREAKDOWN.

His imagination played with the idea that everything was merely a corporate test to measure his patience and reactions. Therefore, he waited resignedly for fifteen minutes, after which he decided to meet his colleagues at the reception. Before that, however, he organised his belongings in a coordinated manner. First, he strategically placed the suitcase in the bathroom; then, the rug and bath towel were set in perfect symmetry in case anyone moved them during his absence; next, a last inspection, and he left. Now he was controlling Big Brother.

While at the bar enjoying a small coffee, a piece of information came: the service technician was waiting for him in his room.

Arriving there, he noticed with a suspicion that the maintenance staff had spotless and neat uniforms. He also realised that one of them was wearing two badges, one of which was from a different hotel. Everything seemed strange to him, including the fact that there were two people to solve a simple matter of resetting a safe password. After a quick analysis, they concluded that they would have to crack open the safe. Feeling annoyed, he opened the bathroom door and noticed the towel had fallen. His conclusion: 'Wow, it is true, they are spying on me; I am in some kind of Big Brother!'

Driving his car to São Paulo, he still felt that he was being followed, even observed, and that his companions were part of the scheme, turning reality into a great piece of fiction by George Orwell. That night, he stayed overnight at his sister's house in Sampa (as people from São Paulo affectionately call their city). Then, he followed his way to his job in the Paraíba Valley on the morning of the following day.

After arriving at the hotel on Friday, he struggled to concentrate and assimilate ideas. Furthermore, he could not focus on the issues discussed with his assistant. She unsuccessfully tried to help him in any possible way she could, but his mind was in a sense of turmoil. The more he tried to understand what was happening, the more confused he became. It felt like distorted radio waves: he tried to remember the computer password but could not; his hands were sweating, his heart was pounding, and he could not recollect any of his passwords. He was definitely losing control.

At that point, he asked the assistant to accompany him to a café in the shopping centre. He needed to confide his concern over an evil plan devised by his French teacher (a charismatic and unsuspecting person with an MBA in Metacognition and Neurolinguistic Programming, who also offered him homemade madeleines regularly) and his financial supervisor. He was sure they were in collusion to divert resources from the hotel! Following his distorted view, the professor had managed to obtain his passwords through mental manipulation and advanced hypnosis techniques.

During coffee, he told his assistant how much he admired her work. However, in his present mental malfunction, he believed she was a special envoy and, along with his girlfriend, was on a mission to investigate the financial crime.

While in the shopping centre, at the same time he was talking to her, he looked attentively in all directions. He meticulously paid attention to everyone in the surroundings of the café, to each passing soul, looking for reference images or people he knew who might be in disguise. He was still under surveillance! There was Carlos, a hotel owner with whom he had worked, walking past them and spying on the conversation from the corner of his eye. He would have to be extra careful. His imagination told him they were sharing state secrets, just like a typical scene from a James Bond film.

Back at the hotel, he sought comfort in his plants. They had a vegetable garden, perhaps the contact with nature would help him, but his efforts were in vain. He had lost control of his mind, and all he could do was cry, his gaze fixed on his beloved jabuticaba tree. That was when he decided to take the car and go back to São Paulo. After all, there was his nephew's birthday party, so he thought a weekend rest and contact with his girlfriend and family would do him well.

On his way to the road, near the hotel corner, he saw a woman lying on the street. What could have happened? Probably a hit-and-run incident. 'I'll change my route', he thought. 'Have I run over the poor thing and denied her assistance?'

'My God, what's happening to me? I can't hesitate; it's getting dark, and I don't feel able to drive to my destination. I'm afraid I have no way out, I need to go, oh my! They're following me, that car parked on the hard shoulder, it's pulled off after I overtook it, they're after me, what can I do?'

He decided to stop at a service station and check the road, but he could no longer see the 'suspicious' car, so he continued his journey. Keeping the speed limit, he expected to be hit by a stone or any object thrown down by robbers any time he crossed a flyover. Almost in a panic, always staring at the rearview mirror and making some unexpected stops to dodge the 'bad guys' who were tailing him, he finally arrived at his sister Glaucia's house. 'Have they already left for the party's venue? I need help. Wait a minute. The cars are still here: good, my mom and sister haven't left yet.'

He asked for help, not knowing what was going on, and when he tried to explain, everything got muddled. How desperate! His mother advised him to go to a spiritist centre nearby for fluid therapy (spiritual treatment with magnetised water). He quickly agreed, and as soon as he stepped into the consoling place, he felt his mind calming down, his ideas becoming clearer. After asking for his name to be added to a list of people requiring help, he proceeded to his beloved nephew's party.

He felt so much better that he scheduled an appointment with the centre's president to come back the following day. His mental confusion led to this decision because the director of the company he worked for had advised him to know his leaders better; he found the same counsel in a book he had been reading. So he had to get complete information about them.

He saw in the spiritist centre president the figure of a spiritual leader who had dedicated his entire life to helping people in need. Furthermore, the man also took care of a nursery for poor children. The following morning, he left the flat to meet this gentleman much earlier than scheduled, so he waited more than an hour. He felt exhausted as he wandered around the neighbourhood in his car, thinking of himself as the bearer of some sacred revelation.

He would only communicate the revelation to the press in the coming week, so he needed the protection of everyone who could help him against the evil forces working incessantly to steal the message. There were rumours that Chico Xavier, the most famous Brazilian medium, had left a password to a trusted person before his death. Whoever unravelled it would be his blessed emissary, irrefutable proof of life after death. Our confused superhero asked for the presence of the spiritual guide; together, they would receive a special prize, and he would soon be famous. He had received the message, and he knew the password. As a result, next Friday would be 'D' day, the day for the press release; also, his personal 'B' day, the breakdown day...

The misfortune continued throughout the weekend, but the big problem would be physical, since he could not disconnect. His brain would not stop working. He schemed creatively, from routine affairs to international plots. He could not sleep or, colloquially speaking, could not sleep a wink. His nephew had been taken to the hospital the night before with a severe bronchitis attack. After making a few phone calls, he got in his car and left the house to see him. Unfortunately, he arrived late, and after staying there for some time, he went out on the streets to register his presence. He stopped at the pharmacy on Heitor Penteado Avenue, one of the main roads in the neighbourhood, and bought some throat pills. It was 2:30 am; he was the revelation's holder and needed to be seen by all.

Returning to his sister's house at 3:30 am, he immediately started to work, regardless of the time. He called friends with whom he had not been in touch for some time and tried to call his girlfriend intermittently. There were some crucial recommendations for her; a list of tasks, including getting money and passports. After publicising the revelation, they would spend some time abroad, possibly in France, to sidestep the media. There would be some enlightening studies while he waited for further information from the summit. Lastly, at 5 am, he called his sister, who had just returned home with her sick son: a call from his mobile while in the same house with her.

'Hello, please add another name to the list.'

'What?' she replied, 'what list are you talking about? Here's your sister, what do you want?

'Oh, that's you... I'm sorry. Have you got Aline's number?'

That was the last straw. Her patience ran out, and, as a result, she sent him to their mother's flat. After all, their mother was responsible for the situation because she had brought such a creature into the world!

He felt more comfortable and protected there, as his sister had been acting strangely, probably because she was serving evil. He could no longer trust her; there you had, another victim in his long list of suspects.

On Saturday afternoon, he asked his girlfriend out. Why not, she thought. Going out around the city to breathe fresh air would benefit him. Everything was coming about nicely when he suddenly decided she should park the car.

'Stop here, now, please!'

They were in the car park of an exquisite chandelier store at Gabriel Monteiro da Silva Avenue, in an upper-class district in São Paulo. He walked into the store, analysing everything as if he were an interior decorator hired by an ultrarich client with a new mansion. After some time, the assistant invites them to visit the upper floor and points to the lift, found in the centre of the store. At this point, he had no choice but to reveal to his girlfriend why they had stopped there: they had to elude the cars following them. Besides, he was sure he would be abducted if they got into the lift, so he suggested running away from the store.

She was perplexed by the revelation but followed him anyway. From the store, they went straight to his mother's flat. His condition was becoming grave, she thought unhappily.

In the early hours of Sunday, his mother decided to take him to the Nove de Julho Hospital for a medical consultation. They arrived there at 4 am; a nurse checked his blood pressure, and the result was not good: 18/12. If he had not had medical assistance, he could have had a heart attack or maybe even a stroke. While they waited for the psychiatrist, it did not take long for the patient to become a doctor, even sitting in his chair. He talked to the nurses on duty, discussing improvements to their routine and work environment.

There was also an incident with some noisy young men accompanying a friend in an alcoholic coma, taking intravenous glucose. Our hero felt he was the authority on duty and immediately scolded the group, stating that they were in a hospital, so they should respect the other patients and 'the party is over'. The silence was soon restored, only to be broken some minutes later when a lady with a broken femur arrived, in intense pain, to the despair of our doctor for a day.

They were still awaiting the psychiatrist, who was attending an emergency in the Albert Einstein Israelite Hospital at that very moment. The waiting was the trigger for our patient to devise another scheme, which included his ex-wife and the psychiatrist. The plot was to commit him to a private clinic for years with an expensive one-way ticket. Afraid of being sedated and hospitalised, he pretended to swallow the pill he was given; instead, he pressed it with the tip of his tongue against his teeth. He then dumped it in a nearby potted plant with a subtle movement while another patient distracted the nurse.

'Great, I'm still in control. Things are working out as planned, and they won't lock me up! Now, I only need to convince the psychiatrist I'm fine. After all, the last months of work were hectic, too stressful, and nothing that some tranquillisers and a good rest couldn't resolve. Maybe going away on holiday.'

His script was well-thought-out and carefully revised. He knew that the more he said, the worse it would be. Avoiding confrontation and stating facts as plainly as possible was crucial because the slightest mistake would be fatal.

At last, the psychiatrist arrived. After twenty minutes of chatting, during which he made a massive effort to follow the script and not *ivulge his secrets, he was me*icate* an* release*. It was 10:30 am. 'Phew, that was close!'*

Already in his mother's flat, they tried to make him sleep, putting him in a dark room. However, our secret agent discovered that he could not control his brain because, when he was about to fall asleep, the telephone would beep, indicating to those outside the room that they could take him to a clinic. At that moment, he decided that sleeping was out of the question and asked to see Malu, his cousin and a psychologist, to come and talk to him. He created a real scene of hostages in reverse, the victims being his family, when the only victim was him, a hostage of himself.

To fool everyone, he went to the bathroom and put on only one of his contact lenses, the right one. He wanted to stay alert and, cunningly, opened a new pair and replaced them into the case. As a result, no one would ever suspect that he was wearing only the right lens.

He determined that his mother's flat should have a 24-hour guard. His mother would take care of the main entrance, and her partner would watch over the bedroom door, while the dog would stay inside with him. He pulled the telephone set from the socket, which, even disconnected, still made some whistling noises. The same was happening with the clock. That was getting ugly; his enemies had cutting-edge technology! He threw the telephone away, which shattered on the floor, ending the eavesdropping. Next, all branded objects with any logo or marketing were torn off and placed into a cloth tube covered with Walt Disney characters, then tucked under a sheet.

He could not tell the revelation to anybody. Whenever someone entered the room without his permission, he would call out his mother's partner, to whom he had given the responsibility for the door safety. He should fulfil his part of the bargain and expel the intruder. Not even his sister and girlfriend were allowed into the bedroom. Eventually, his cousin arrived, and the negotiations started.

He felt he could tell her the valid reason behind his actions and discuss the scheme. However, there was not enough time, so he developed an exceedingly intelligent conversation system: when wearing glasses, he needed to know the therapist's opinion; when taking them off, he wanted to speak. His personality entirely changed with each removal of the glasses, and he could hold an agile conversation this way.

He told Malu everything, including his method for controlling the days remaining until the revelation. He had put a clock in the centre of a shelf, flanked by small owls from his mother's collection. The birds would then be moved from the right side of the clock to the left one at each daybreak. That way, he would not miss the date and the subsequent meeting with authorities, including Luiz Inácio Lula da Silva, the country's president at that time[4].

He realised things were coming to a head when the doctor from the Nove de Julho Hospital tried to get into the bedroom. Moreover, he peeped through the door crack and saw other people trying to come in; sure, they were doctors and nurses. An easy conclusion, as they were all dressed in white from neck to toe, 'maybe even white pants', he thought. At this point, he panicked, persuading himself that they would put him in a straitjacket and hospitalise him for a long time under periodic electroshock sessions. He could not understand such injustice. Everything he had done was for a noble cause. But, unfortunately, evil was win-

---

4. TN – In 2004, Mr Lula da Silva was serving his first term as president. He was reelected in 2006 and, after winning the 2022 general election, he was sworn in on 1 January 2023

ning, and they were all traitors, including his cousin! Presently, he was terrified.

The doctor and the therapist had a long talk with him. Then, finally, they told him he had two options: being hospitalised or allowing them to give him an injection. Naturally, he opted for the second one, but not without stating his outrage: it was unacceptable that, well into the 21st century, humanity still resorted to injectable drugs, an excruciating and traumatic method!

There was a clear and imminent danger: he would become unconscious after the injection, and they would send him to a clinic. At long last, he let them give him the medication, an injection of haloperidol (an antipsychotic drug); he had thrown in the towel.

His cousin left the room, and he had the opportunity to talk to the doctor, finding out that he had Jewish ancestry. Our failed hero had strong personal connections with Israel. He visited the country in the 1990s (Eilat, Jerusalem, Haifa). Besides, his father had written the Jewish review for several years. He started his professional life at Editora Abril, a well-known Brazilian publishing company, and he met Mr Victor Civita, the company founder. Mr Civita was a Jewish journalist, an Italo-Brazilian whose family migrated from Italy to New York in 1938.

However, his worst scare was about to come: the bedroom door opened, and through it came the nurse, a massive figure almost as wide as the door itself. Of course, it would take anyone a great deal of visual-spatial ability to imagine such a character inside the room, more or less like playing Tetris on an advanced level: one should accommodate a five-seater L-shaped sofa inside a building's lift. But, facing reality, he decided to collaborate with his relocation and offered a quiet rendition. After all, he was freaking out but had not gone nuts!

He was placed into the ambulance with no recollection of having got there. His sister, however, remembers having seen him calmly leaving the flat, walking backwards, accompanied by the doctor and the nurses from the clinic.

Then, his memory resumed, and things started to become clear again. He remembered that he had been an eyewitness to the 11 September attacks in New York, so the kind doctor was, in fact, a secret agent serving Israel.

Indeed, it all made sense now. Our hero had been the victim of an international plot led by Afghans under the coordination of Osama bin Laden. During his trip to Israel and Egypt years ago, someone brainwashed him, perhaps microchipped him, and instructed his subconscious to engage in terrorist acts years later, the ones that changed the world forever.

He could see the connection with the dinner the President of Senegal gave in honour of Her Majesty Queen Elisabeth at the Royal Automobile Club in 1998. He was working there at that time.

That is why he visited the Twin Towers only on Sunday, two days before the attack. It was apparent they would kill him inside the ambulance!

At that moment, he felt cold and scared and fell into a deep sleep.

11 September 2001

11 September 2001

'Lex Luthor, Superman's archenemy, managed to steal four aeroplanes and launched them against targets in Metropolis and the Capital. Fortunately, the Man of Steel (Superman himself) managed to take down one of them before it reached its target. However, the remaining ones were successful. One hit the US Intelligence Agency and the other two brought down the biggest financial centre in Metropolis. That was an enormous victory for evil. However, the Justice League is ready to punish Luthor and his thugs. Superman, Batman, and their companions have already found the villains' hideout and their allies will pay. America mourns its dead.'

Source: www.klpsidra.net;27/05/04

Our man was in Metropolis on the day of the WTC attack. That is, he was in New York on 11 September 2001. He had been in the Big Apple for a week, and his home journey would happen on the exact date of the attacks. On this trip, he accompanied a starred Chef on a gastronomic tour that included visiting hotels. That was what he was doing at the time of the attacks. He had an appointment with the sales manager at the Hudson Hotel, at 356 West 58th Street, near Ninth Avenue. Philipe Starck, Anda Andrei and Ian Schrager were at 58th Street for the recreation of the Hudson, the latest acquired property of Schrager's hotel group, opened in the autumn of 2000, with one thousand apartments.

Built in 1928 by J.P. Morgan's daughter, the Hudson had gone through some peculiar changes. Ten previous floors were set apart to the St. Luke's Hospital and transformed into dormitories. Ten additional ones became the Channel Thirteen Headquarters, including the office and production studio. Finally, in 1997, the ISH group bought the property. Three years and USD 125 million later, its doors reopened as the Hudson.

When approaching the exposed brick building, the impression was of an old American high school. The unpretentious doors opened into a low ceiling foyer leading to two escalators rising nine metres. The feeling was of entering a tunnel. One could see the sky through the lobby's glass ceiling upon arrival. The reception area displayed a thirteen-metre-long table of solid oak, carved in France, and assembled in the hotel as part of the Art Nouveau inspiration.

The reception was an authentic urban conservatory, warm and inviting, full of rustic bricks, dark wood, and a selection of vines climbing more than nine metres high, reaching a glass ceiling. French doors led to a terrace filled with plants, oversized furniture, and an unconventional sculpture. On the mezzanine and third floor, the hotel offered several function rooms. The library was equally outstanding: there were engravings of cows parading and hats from the latest Chanel's collection; also, many floor-to-ceiling seven-metre-high shelves stacked with books. Finally, a pool table.

In the restaurant, enormous wooden benches, as if on a farm, were shared by guests and customers, all amazed by the chefs' culinary skills while preparing sublime food. He was fascinated, trying to assimilate these stunning environments, masterpieces by Philipe Stark, worth admiring. Minimalistic, futuristic, contemporary, unconventional: Starck, a genius.

Realising it was past the appointment time with the hotel manager, he immediately went to the reception and presented himself:

'Please, I have an appointment with the sales manager, supposed to be at 9 o'clock. Unfortunately, I'm flying today, so I don't have much time. Could you please check what time she will be here?'

The receptionist looked me straight in the eye and asked:

'Don't you know what happened just now?' as if she were talking to someone who had just arrived from another planet.

'No, what?' I asked with a detached expression.

'An aeroplane crashed into the WTC some minutes ago, and it appears that another one has just crashed.' the girl replied, looking relieved to tell me.

'The WTC, the Twin Towers? One plane and then another?' I reiterated, in disbelief, to make sure I had understood the message.

'Yes, exactly. We have an observatory on the top floor. Would you like to see it from there?'

'Yes, certainly. How do I get there?' I asked, expelling the air from my lungs, in a mixture of 'can I?' with 'let's go!'.

When I arrived at the terrace, I disbelieved the apoc-alyptic scene: the massive towers that defined the city skyline burning in smoke. So, I rubbed my eyes with the tip of my fingers, closed them, lowered my head, opened them again and fixed my gaze toward the buildings. I could distinguish the gigantic towers being swallowed by the fire, and I could see a smoke screen that stretched for miles above them and a huge black stain covering the entire length of the façade on the highest floors.

My brain was in denial and couldn't register what I was seeing. It was like watching a film, a surreal scene!

Looking around, I noticed a guy near me filming. He seemed to be a TV camera operator carrying profes-sional equipment. I asked him:

'What happened?', still unbelieving, heart and soul.

'Terrorist attack', he replied.

'My God, this is war' was my first thought. What was I doing there? Maybe there were chemical weapons on the planes that attacked the towers, and we would all fry there.

I went to the ground floor as fast as I could. Then, leaving the hotel, I started walking towards the towers, reaching more or less the distance of twenty blocks from what became known as 'ground zero'. I entered the first deli shop I saw, bought a disposable camera, and wan-dered devastated through the fenced streets. There were police officers with megaphones, alone or in pairs, giving instructions to the crowd roaming across the area, trying to understand what had happened.

I saw dozens of ambulances, firefighters, and police cars going at high speed towards the towers; cars leaving the scene entirely covered in soot or something like lime. There were also people covered in the same substance, dust, ashes, smoke, coughing, trying to catch their breath, and being helped by the locals.

I approached a group of people. Some were crying desperately. Friends were hugging each other with tears in their eyes, helpless people watching in disbelief at what seemed like the end of the world. Then, after a short time, someone started screaming that the tower would fall. This time, it was the collapse of the north tower.

We all watched the smoke of the tower change, taking on the mushroom shape, the ominous sign of a nuclear detonation, and the whole building began to crash like a cascade of dominoes.

It took 11 seconds for the 110-story colossus to fall to the ground, killing thousands of human beings who, on that fateful 11 September 2001, just wanted to go on with their lives. Instead, the area became 'the biggest crime scene in the world', with bodies and the smell of burning.

Smothering air, the sweet smell of burning that churns the stomach and enters the body through the nose, sticking to the throat.

The sadness, the horror: the most significant symbol of capitalism and of the greatest empire on the planet was destroyed. Hearts torn apart, desolation, innocent lives lost, disbelief added to the smell of death, there was no longer a safe place in the world. I sat on the pavement and cried.

We got stuck in New York for another five days and saw the city completely transform. Phone calls were impossible, and no public transport was available to take us back to the Delmonico Hotel on Park Avenue, where we were staying. The underground service stopped, and the streets were overwhelmed by people trying to get a taxi or bus, all already stuck in traffic, mobile networks down. The sound of fire alarms from the neighbouring buildings, adding to car alarms and ambulance sirens, was maddening! We worried about getting accommodation during the calamity, more than a bit of concern, as the airspace was closed. Nobody on the island would leave it. We walked from Greenwich Village to the Delmonico Hotel[5].

Upon arriving at the hotel, we learnt about the death toll climbing to six thousand. However, authorities would know the actual number only days later. At that moment, the rumour mill was confusing and panicking the population.

The following day, the authorities issued stay-at-home orders, so we could not leave the hotel. Only the emergency services were allowed to go around the city. The Empire State Building

---

5. AN - The Delmonico is part of New York City's history. It opened its door at 502 Park Avenue on the corner of 59th Street in 1928, and thus before the Great Stock Market Crash of 1929. After the 9/11 attacks, it was purchased by the millionaire Donald Trump for USD 115 million, being renamed 'Trump Park Avenue'. Remodelling began soon after, costing USD 80 million to transform it into a high-end property. Completed in 2004, the building has a duplex penthouse with 42 large windows that was priced then at a paltry sum of USD30 million.

was evacuated three times because of false bomb alarms. People could hear all kinds of information; in fact, nobody knew what was happening.

On the third day after the attacks, we were finally allowed to leave the hotel, and we noticed a massive presence of police officers and army members on every corner of New York. The airspace was still closed, but military planes always flew. I also noted that the hotel bellhop was not wearing his badge, so I asked him why.

'My name is Mohamed, sir. What do you think will happen to me?'

It was hideous to realise people were going utterly crazy, the stories of xenophobia spreading throughout the city. We learnt that people in car parks ran over anyone wearing a veil. There was the story of the Brazilian taxi driver who was mistaken for an Arab and had to prove his nationality to a group of threatening young men. Unfortunately, some impetuous individuals wanted to take the law into their hands, criminally acting against innocent people, who were victims as much as any of us on the Island of death.

Each year on the anniversary of the 9/11 attacks, I would pick up the phone and call my friend Antonio Faustino de Oliveira, also known as Chef Russo. I wanted to remind him of the day we had made the best decision of our lives: to visit the towers on Sunday instead of Tuesday. It would have been the twenty-first call this year had he not died on 4 April 2010, aged 45, a victim of a massive heart attack. Rest in peace, my dear friend.

For now, enough of this atrocious episode. It has already traumatised our character very much.

It was 17 September when he arrived in Brazil.

On 30 September, he separated from his wife, a painful decision based on irreconcilable differences. When dividing their common assets, meaning a couple of poodles named Kalu and Whiskey, he kept Whiskey. The dog, not the bottle. Anyway, as Vinicius de Moraes[6] said, Whiskey is man's best friend, so there you are, a bottled dog! Unfortunately, his little friend was run over a short time later in his building's shared area.

He carried the animal's body from the accident site to the cold stainless-steel table of the veterinary clinic. He suffered a lot with the loss of his faithful squire. Poor creature!

And on 30 November, he was dismissed from his job.

Had Bin Laden come to Brazil in his suitcase???

In less than three months, our friend was separated, devoid of Whiskey and available on the job market. Everything happened in sequence and caused long after-effects, long severe after-effects.

---

6. TN – Vinicius de Moraes was a famous Brazilian poet and composer. He was one of the authors of 'Girl from Ipanema'.

CHILDHOOD AND ANCESTRY

Childhood

Wow, what a relief to be dreaming. Our man is back to his childhood, a street scamp, always up to no good, climbing walls like a cat. His mother had to take him to the hospital every week: once, he had stitches in his head while still having some on the nose from an earlier incident a few days before. The scamp was thus compared to Emilia, the rag doll from 'Sítio do Picapau Amarelo' by Monteiro Lobato[7]. Mother would take him to get the stitches, but after so many comings and goings, she learnt to take them out herself.

After the daily shower, his father would place him on top of the toilet lid to smear him with mercurochrome. With so many shenanigans, there was almost no visible space on his snow-white skin: the boy looked like a walking beet. The little devil had had a penchant for speed since he was six months old. His sister would take him for rides in a wheelbarrow, and she had to speed it up; otherwise, he would cry like a weaned goat. Perhaps he carried experiences from earlier lives because he could not stand the sight of a wheelchair. If he happened to see one, a real drama would ensue, like a trauma without an actual cause.

On the other hand, his passion for travelling had a clear explanation. His father was a fashion journalist, and going to Paris and Milan every year was mandatory. So, the trips to the old Vi-

---

7. TN - 'Sítio do Picapau Amarelo'(literally translated as The Yellow Woodpecker Farm) is a series of 23 fantasy novels written by Monteiro Lobato (1882/1948). In the story, Emilia is a living rag doll famous for her mischiefs

racopos airport in Campinas (São Paulo state), whose floor had chequered tiles, became engraved on his mind. He was always fascinated by the novelties brought by their parents, ecstatic when they opened the luggage. He could smell Europe, and everything was so different! At that time, distances seemed larger; there was no internet or social media. The fastest connection was called telex, and snail mail took days to arrive. Digital systems as we know them today were unheard of, and the electronic era was still at a crawl. The world was more delimited, meaning more unconnected and less globalised.

His first international trip was to Paraguay at the age of ten. How could he ever forget it? When they were about to board the plane, the inseparable bag with his collection of scale model cars came loose, and the kid had to pick up all the little pieces of his treasure scattered on the runway. He was helped by his sister and the other passengers, all on alert to the landings and take-offs. Unfortunately, only his father was travelling with them. At that time, their parents were going through a separation process. The fact was traumatic for the boy, who was very attached to his dad, his superhero.

The father once told a childhood friend, called Maria Alice, that he could not erase from his memory the sadness of the moment of the separation. It was a winter day with an intermittent drizzle. By nightfall, the house already empty, he said goodbye to his children, who were departing to live with their grandparents. Soon after, all alone, he turned the lights off, looked again into the deserted house, locked the door and left aimlessly, taking only the clothes he was wearing, a suitcase and a broken heart. He was leaving behind his home and a large part of his life.

His father indeed carried the burden of a traumatic relationship with his mother. Maria Alice, with whom the boy kept in touch and became like a second mother to him, recalled an odd occasion at the primary school where they studied. One day, a lady came to pick up the friend and his brother, and Maria asked him who she was. No one, he replied, just a family acquaintance. Later on, talking to his friend's brother, she learnt that the lady was, in fact, their mother.

What had possibly happened?

Why did the boy deny his mother?

Not even his wife, during the eighteen years of their marriage, came to know why her husband avoided his mother. They had not seen each other for over twenty-five years. The lady, desperate and longing, asked her not to answer the phone at a specific time of the day. She would then call their number to hear her son's voice without saying a word—a silent call, with the only purpose of hearing the sound of his voice.

Back to his childhood

It was the seventies, and being a separated woman was still objectionable. So, Grandpa Guilhermino insisted they lived in his home, a simple house with two bedrooms and only one bathroom. It was, however, the Headquarters of the whole family, and everybody would gather there, dozens of members.

The boy shared a room with his mother and sister, while the grandparents kept the front room. There was a dog, a French poodle, with pedigree and all, including a surname: Alex de Beaumont. But they had to donate Onassis, their beautiful white Persian cat, when they moved. There was not enough room for everybody in the new home.

Grandpa Guilhermino, a Portuguese born in Trás-os-Montes and naturalised Brazilian, was the one who kept the entire family together. Soon after moving to his house, the kid developed a strong bond of affection with him. Guilhermino was a man of wisdom, a counsellor. Despite limited schooling and having only primary education, he was a self-learner, able to talk about any subject with authority, particularly politics. His pet peeve was people who still wrote Brasil with zed[8].

Undoubtedly, Grandpa's influence represented the beginning of his love for gastronomy. For the older man, a meal should be complete: soup, salad, main course, and lots of fruit. So, he would bring flavoursome fruit from Ceagesp[9] once a week and equally distribute them among his three daughters.

As the boy only saw his father during weekends, Guilhermino made up for his lack of a father figure. Then, one day, he overheard a conversation between grandpa and his mother, in which the older man mentioned his routine cardiac tests had indicated a problem. From what the boy understood, he had an enlarged heart, which sounded severe. Crying, the child got the savings the grandfather would give him as payment for running errands and bought him some limes for the caipirinha[10]. Guilhermino, with teary eyes, hugged him and said he was delighted because it was the first time a grandchild had bought him something.

One afternoon, after lunch with the family, the grandfather sat in his armchair for his usual nap. The boy sat on the floor, leaning against his grandfather's legs, who was sleeping soundly by then. Suddenly, his grandmother, who had walked past them towards the kitchen, came back and started shaking him, calling out his name, trying to wake him up, to no avail. At that moment, she asked her son-in-law to assist with the resuscitation

---

8. TN – Until 1931, the country's official name was written with zed. The change was a consequence of the Portuguese Language Agreement of that year.
9. TN – A company where people and food suppliers can buy horticultural products.
10. TN – Caipirinha is a famous Brazilian drink made with cachaça (sugar cane spirit), lime, white sugar, and ice.

procedure; the uncle shouted to the boy and told him to go to the nearby clinic to ask for help and get them to send an ambulance urgently. The boy ran through the streets as fast as he could, but his efforts were in vain: his beloved grandad had already passed away.

Grandpa was only sixty-nine years old. He left this world still young, but it was the way he always said he wanted it: 'sleeping and with a full belly.' Be that as it may, he left an immense emptiness in his grandson, who suffered a lot. So not only had Guilhermino been missed as a grandfather, but he had also been the boy's surrogate father.

Guilhermino's death and his parents' separation, still uncommon in the 70s, certainly left wounds in all of them.

Hospitalisation

As I imagined during the talks in the bedroom at my mother's flat, I became unconscious after the inevitable injection and was taken to a clinic. But, you see, an insane person also knows stuff. What I didn't realise was that they would forget to blanket me. The megadose of tranquilliser wasn't enough to drop me unconscious, nor was I insensitive to the cold. And I was freezing!

There was an alternation between being unconscious and aware of the rescue in the icy ambulance, snow monster and all. God, I had never felt so cold before; it was dreadful. Besides beating my brain out for days, I was now undoubtedly chattering my teeth. And still, nobody had a bit of common sense to care about me. This experience has to belong very high on my list of dislikes, on which injections and wheelchairs are at the top.

Because of the excessive medication dose, I cannot recall the moment we arrived at the clinic. I only have a memory of waking up at some point in a small room, lying, my head resting on my girlfriend's lap. My mother was there, and a dear friend who at that time was the Human Resources manager at the company I worked. The room was almost devoid of furniture: only a dark-coloured two-seater sofa and a trolley. I felt neither fear nor cold, just bewilderment and doubt. It was Sunday, 2 May, around 5 pm.

When I woke up again, fourteen hours had passed. I looked around and realised I was in a ward with twelve beds, all occupied by men and women.

I missed my mother. My trolley was next to a small workstation in the centre of the room, where a nurse was working. I could hear screams; people were moving restlessly, and some were babbling and wandering around, always followed by the watchful eyes of three nurses. I said I needed to go to the bathroom, and one of them pointed the way. So, I sat up on the trolley, looking for my things. A nurse immediately handed me a pair of shoes kept under the mattress to avoid getting lost. I went to the bathroom, perturbed by the place's simplicity, and also frightened by the disorientated comportment of the people there. There was widespread anxiety in the air, which I picked up on there and then. It was as if I were observing everything from afar, not belonging but still with utter apprehension.

I returned to my bed and resignedly waited, yet still observantly. Finally, a nurse offered me a tray with breakfast. Then, I heard a doctor, who sounded Asian, comment that they would soon transfer me from intensive care.

It was a 'damn' moment: I was in a clinic and, on top of that, in the Intensive Care Unit! Mine was a severe case. Surprisingly, I perceived that something distinct was occurring. On other occasions, under the same circumstances, I would have been desperate. But, nevertheless, I felt calmer, as if I were controlling the situation. Was that feeling a result of the tranquillisers? Or something else entirely?

I had breakfast leaning against the nurse's desk. Although I was not a coffee-with-milk person, I had no choice but to swallow it. I also ate some cornstarch biscuits that were wrapped in half a napkin.

I knew my journey would be of considerable length; therefore, I had to feed myself. During breakfast, I was under the impression of somehow being spared from interference. My feeling was of some protection, like an invisible bubble that kept the ambient noise and the patients' voices from reaching me: a pastoral tranquillity, the silence of God. Soon after, they removed me from the ICU. A nurse accompanied me, showing me the clinic's facilities.

We walked past some half-open doors, and I saw patients sleeping in their beds. Soon after leaving the women's ward, we reached our destination: a room with three low dark wood beds, all with thin mattresses, and two shared bathrooms opposite. Two beds were occupied; the free one was the closest to the door on the left.

The place was plain and unadorned. The wardrobes were just wooden boxes with doors, nailed to the wall. Red tiles covered the floor, and the only window, which was next to my bed, had bars. There was nothing else in the room. It opened to the corridor and, almost opposite, a shared bathroom.

The person in the nearest bed was under deep sedation. He had had a hard blow to his head due to a fight. His name was Leto, and he was 45 years old. He remained sedated for the next few days but had some lucid moments when he was very friendly and coherent. I must have slept for the next eight hours, waking up when my mother and sister came to see me around 2 pm; it was visiting hours. I was delighted to see them: we held hands, and I realised how essential family affection is in difficult times. They mean unconditional love. I felt enormous relief, as there were no more conspiracies nor enemies, only my beloved family.

I wanted to get up, but I was yet under the effect of the drugs. Still, I tried and went to the bathroom to shower. My mother had brought me shampoo, soap, clean clothes, and a spiritist book.

Leto's wife and daughters also came, and their presence immediately transformed him. The happiness of seeing them was visible and gave him the strength to work on recovering. We both seemed like cars being filled up at petrol stations, only our fuel was family love. But unfortunately, upon returning from the shower, I noticed no visits for the patient next to Leto. I cried, thinking how difficult it would be to endure such a challenging situation without family support.

There was a strict observation of the visiting hours' rules, so when the time was over, I felt like leaving with them. That was when I truly realised, I was confined. But how come? I was not crazy after all, only a little confused.

At that moment, I understood that nothing happens by chance: I was in that clinic to get help and help others in a worse situation than mine. That was, indeed, a learning opportunity, one that stimulated me to face the facts. I decided to get to know people better because we were in the same boat. One of the first things I noticed was that, aside the simplicity of the place, everyone here was very considerate, particularly the nurses.

They carefully distributed little coffee cups with the name of the patients on trays (and, in them, their medication), in the men's ward, inside a room next to ours.

I took my medicines dutifully twice daily, without pretending or spitting them out. After the medication, I participated in a very eclectic group therapy on the first day. There were men and women of different ages, and I concentrated on hearing everybody, including the therapist. The activity consisted of pair work: we had a blank sheet of paper on which we had to draw lines alternating different colours, one of us continuing the line of the other until filling the entire sheet length within a time limit.

Gilberto Gil, a famous Brazilian composer and singer, once wrote a song called 'Sandra' about his wife, and other women he met during a short stay in a psychiatric hospital. (I recommend listening to it.) My partner in the activity was also called Sandra, and she was swift in her gestures and train of thought. She seemed faster than I was, as if running at a higher voltage. We completed our task before the other groups, and after the circumscriptions, we had to find figures or things in the drawings; ours was also the one with the highest number of shapes found. The other pairs' presentation made the individual members' distinct pathology clear.

In a way, I found the exercise positive. Overall, there was contact with the female patients, who were kept in separate areas from us, except for group therapy and meals. Furthermore, the therapist conducted the session very professionally: she brought the dispersive patients back to the activity and integrated the group naturally. There were some sofas where the therapy group worked, and I enjoyed sitting there for my daily reading. It was a pleasant area, with a view of the plants in the garden. On the second day, while I was reading, the therapist came into the room with a different group and invited me to participate. I readily agreed.

'One moment', she said. 'It seems your name is not on the list of today's group.' The right thing to do was leave the room, so I did. The scene repeated on the third day, but I immediately declined the invitation. I assumed they would find me if I were supposed to take part in the session.

We had four meals a day: breakfast, lunch, afternoon snack and dinner, and all served in the dining hall, which consisted of six tables for four people and one long table for about twelve people. I usually sat at the smaller tables, as I preferred to be with the people from my closest group. Unfortunately, the thermos bottles had no identification; so, it was hard to tell them apart, whether it was coffee, milk or tea, and we inquired among ourselves to learn their contents. The food was good, although the kitchen's staff service left something to be desired, as they used plastic bowls to distribute the required amount on our plates.

I started to have digestive problems, like heartburn and stomach burning. The doctor prescribed antacids, and soon I felt better. However, we were always hungry, perhaps because of the medicines and the fact that there was no exercise routine.

The garden was my favourite place in the clinic. There were several trees, among them a jabuticaba and a fantastic bougainvillaea. We could reach it through glass doors in the television room, which also led to the swimming pool. I led a group of five patients, namely the five musketeers, and we played a truth-or-dare game to learn more about each other. We asked personal questions such as: How did they get there? Were they married and had children? What did they do for a living? Had they been hospitalised before?

We created nicknames because everyone, without exceptions, needed help keeping information related to names. Thus, I was 'the Guy from the hotel', and there were 'the Postman', 'the Philosopher', 'the Pastor', 'Big James', 'the Ferrari' (who arrived dressed from head to toe in red, bringing with him a steering wheel with the company logo), among others.

Some of them were real characters! Take the Postman, for instance: he would sweep the outside area and even clean the plant pots, removing the cigarette butts. He would not say a word, only sweeping non-stop. One day I decided to help him with the dustpan, and, as a result, he exchanged a couple of words with me from then on.

Many patients were smokers, and, because of that, the air in the TV room was always brimming with tobacco smoke, so thick you could cut it with a knife. I took it upon myself to check the air quality, so I would open the doors often to allow fresh air. Some of the inmates were there due to drug addiction or alcoholism, hence the reason for so many smokers. It was a logical conclusion considering that bad habits go hand in hand. Returning to our five musketeers group's subject, we organised a morning exercise routine: walks from the backyard to the swimming pool, tracing sinuous paths with imaginary obstacles. Although we talked a lot during the walks, the group got smaller with each passing day.

Every morning we went through an evaluation with the psychologist for about twenty minutes when she questioned us to assess the evolution of the individual situations. During these sessions, we would receive information about our discharge; for this reason, they were a moment of great tension, resulting either in disappointment or relief. And so, we led our lives as inmates in expectation of who would be the next one to cross the clinic's gates. Some were overly anxious about the probability of leaving the place as quickly as possible and, therefore, could not contain themselves.

I have to confess that I also wanted to leave, but I tried very hard not to show my desire, given that any trace of anxiety would get a high negative score on the evaluation for discharge.

One morning, I noticed that Leto was missing during breakfast and immediately ran towards our room. As I had imagined, he was still asleep, so I tried to wake him up. It was not easy, however, because of the medication. In the end, I carried him to the refectory. It was one of the many lessons I learnt during my stay in the clinic: the supportive and caring spirit was a constant in the group. We were one for all and all for one.

If we noticed that someone from the group was missing, one of us, anyone, perhaps the one with whom that person had more contact, would promptly find them and help them in any possible way.

Big James was the group's singer. He organised singing sessions with a very eclectic repertoire, which were always enjoyable. But, unfortunately, during one of these sessions, I relapsed: 'Big Brother' came back when people started to sing 'Enquanto houver sol'[11], whose lyrics had always touched me deeply and had plenty to do with the crisis I was experiencing. It was the same song and verses used in the manager's meeting workshop when it all began.

Consequently, the doctor had to increase the medication dose, which brought the fear of breaking down again. I soon learnt that this fear would follow me for a long time, as it is part of the cure.

I do not quite remember the reason for Big James' hospitalisation. But, if I am correct, it was connected with the stress generated by his college exams and maybe some drug involvement.

The Pastor presented a compelling case. Upon returning from his job as a security guard at around 11 pm, he found a group of beggars at the underground station, started preaching to them and completely forgot to go home. Because he had been previously hospitalised before, his wife contacted the po-

11. 'As long as the sun shines' is a song by a famous Brazilian band called Titãs.

52

lice without hesitation. His case was dramatic: he had a newborn daughter and no other family members in São Paulo. He rarely had visitors because his wife did not have enough money for transport nor with whom to leave the child.

The Philosopher's case, on the other hand, was different. A hard drugs user in his youth, he was a huge fan of Janis Joplin, the Beatles, the Rolling Stones, and Jovem Guarda[12], among others. Back in 1968, he used everything, including injectable drugs. He always carried a Bible with him, using it to preach. So, when he saw I was reading a spiritist novel, he immediately warned me: 'This thing sucks, come off it!'

I felt better with every passing day. Yet, whenever I saw people who somehow reminded me of past events, I would tell myself that everything was just a game, so I continued the battle against my personal 'Truman Show'.

Anyway, I noticed that the amount of medication gradually decreased; I felt more and more alert and ready to help those still struggling. I was finally discharged on Thursday, altogether five days of hospitalisation. My anxiety reached an all-time high, not only because I was leaving but also because two friends from our group still did not know when they would be allowed to leave. I said goodbye to them, thanked the nurses and people with whom I had direct contact, and left.

So I was back to the real world, the world of the less insane, better saying, the almost crazy: their sanity hanging by a thread, on the verge of a breakdown, future patients yet to be diagnosed. I left the clinic on Thursday and returned on Saturday. But do not worry, my dear reader, I did not take an ambulance this time.

---

12. TN – 'Jovem Guarda', roughly translated as 'Young Guard', was a Brazilian music movement that started around the 60s and was influenced by American and British bands of that time.

I went back to visit friends. I was happy to hear that the Pastor had just left and to see Leto again. He was the last from our group and felt pleased with my visit. I was introduced to two new interns, a journalist, and a flight attendant who worked for a major airline.

As we walked through the garden, I saw one of the patients I knew with his girlfriend. He worked as a mechanic in a car manufacturer and had been in the clinic for some time for a strict hypoglycaemic diet under psychological supervision. 'I thank you for not forgetting us', he said. 'Take good care of yourself.'

I said goodbye to everyone and proceeded to the gate, where I was admonished: 'Former patients should not return.' Alright, message acknowledged: 'I will stay away.' But then I left with the awkward sensation of leaving behind something that would be with me forever.

Medicines and Healing

Medicines and Healing

Song 'Epitaph' - Titās

I should have loved more

I should have cried more

I should have seen the sunrise

I should have taken more chances

And even made more mistakes

I should have done what I wanted to do

I would like to have accepted people

As they are

Each person knows the happiness

And the pain they carry in their hearts

Fortune will protect me

As long as I walk absent-mindedly

Fortune will protect me

As long as I walk

I should have complicated less

Worked less

I should have seen the sunset

I should have cared less

About small problems

I should have died of love

I would like to have accepted

Life as it is

It is up to each one the joy

And sadness that happen

In my case, healing occurred in three ways:

- medicines,

- change of habits and

- philosophy and mystic-spiritualism.

Treatment time: five years through a personal and non-transferable journey.

1. Medicines

Apart from the medication I took during the breakdown and at the clinic, here is the routine I followed:

Morning:

- Tic-tac-toe - one pill after breakfast

- 'Red stripe'

Night:

- *The green one - one pill before sleep*

- *'Black stripe'*

- *The orange one - one pill before sleep*

- *'Re• stripe'*

Side effects I felt

- Memory lapse issues and cognitive ability decline,

- communication difficulties,

- mood swings,

- lethargy and lack of vigour,

- social isolation,

- unwillingness to engage in various activities and,

- in my case, a mild depression.

I was fearful that it would happen again. In which case, what would be the risk of another psychotic breakdown? This question kept popping up in my head, bringing a lot of insecurity: I knew the consequences of delusions and losing my mind. This feeling was comparable to the insecurity I felt when living in Mexico. The threat of the next earthquake was constant with daily ground motions, but when would the next big one come? The clinic's doctor said that it could have been an isolated episode because of my age and the kind of breakdown I had.

Nevertheless, he recommended that I check my sleep. This tip helped me a lot: at least it was under my control, and I have paid close attention to my sleep until today, years after the episode. Overall, it has worked out well.

Natural remedies

- *'Rescue' – four ⸱rops four times a ⸱ay; I took ten ⸱rops at the beginning of the treatment.*

- *Laven⸱er essential oil – three ⸱rops on the pillow before sleep.*

- *Rosemary essential oil – temple massaging in the morning.*

- *Flui⬧ therapy once a week.*

- Inspiring readings

- *Pray an⬧ watch*

Follow-up care

I started a psychiatric treatment. The doctor and I opted for 'brief psychotherapy' and continued with the medication prescribed by the clinic's doctor. Brief psychotherapy is an educational therapy focused on the present without ignoring the past and, in addition, considering that people build themselves through their life experiences: what they think and feel and how they behave at the present moment. It is a treatment with a specific focus, a determined period and a goal to develop.

I went to the doctor's practice and explained why I was seeking psychological help. After talking, we both agreed on the number of sessions and the specific problem we would discuss, naming my psychotic breakdown[13] and its possible causes. In my case, I had had delusional disorder symptoms; additionally, there was a possibility I also had bipolar disorder. However, further medical examination, including a head CT (computerised tomography), did not indicate any abnormality, so the doctor ruled out this cause.

In the brief focal psychotherapy, we had weekly 50-minute meetings; in my case, the whole process should last from four to six months. During the sessions, the psychiatrist invited me to talk about the issues that caused suffering, such as financial

---

13. AN - During a psychotic episode, a person's thoughts and perceptions are disturbed, and the individual may experience signs and symptoms such as mental confusion, delusions, hallucinations, catatonia, disorganised and incoherent speech, mood swings, and loss of sense of time, among others.

instability, family conflicts, low self-esteem, professional dissatisfaction and personal dilemmas.

2. Habit changes and learning

Things I have been working on: writing a diary; being close to family members, especially those with whom I have affinities, and listening to them; contacting friends is a priority, but being careful concerning those who are stressed; working too hard is off limits; dogs are essential; having a healthier diet: reducing red meat, coffee, soft drinks, milk and dairy products; having light meals in the evening; taking regular walks, if possible in a park in contact with nature; listening to music, but careful with hardcore music when stressed; changing routines and thinking outside the box; hugging a tree and walking barefoot; reading; pay attention to the surroundings; laughing more, even at myself; observe other people's reactions; do not get involved; looking in the mirror, looking deep in detail into my eyes; see through my body: see my soul and my state of mind.

3. Philosophy[14]

Healing, as we have seen, can happen in three ways:

- Wait for nature to take its course

- Help nature with diet and

- Intervene in the patient's body to restore balance.

One of the essential ideas of ancient medicine is about the diseases' origin and treatment. Their cause comes from the 'physis' (nature) of the patient that correlates with necessity or 'anan-

14. 14. TN – The following text is based on two books by Marilena Chauí, a philosopher and writer from Brazil. 'Introdução à História da Filosofia' and 'Dos Pré-Socráticos a Aristóteles' were published by Companhia das Letras.

ke' (inevitable and unavoidable destiny decided by the gods), resulting in a chronic condition. There is not much a doctor can do apart from alleviating the patient's pain with medicine, in the worst crises, and recommending a permanent diet that helps to compensate for any imbalance of the patient's nature.

On the other hand, medical art is fully requested by diseases whose causes are not by necessity but by accident, that is, diseases caused by a fortuitous encounter between the patient's body and external conditions contrary to his 'physis'. Because he deals, above all, with the accidental, with what belongs to 'tykhe' (fortune, chance), the doctor's task is challenging. And he needs to possess a quality that does not depend only on the knowledge he has accumulated through learning and experience: he needs to be endowed with metis.

Metis is the god who personifies practical intelligence: ingenuity and cunning to solve difficulties, prudence, ingenuity to face a complicated situation, and devising ruses and traps. Whoever possesses it, also possesses the sight that allows grasping the 'kairos', which means the just measure and exact moment because, otherwise, the action may not succeed and will fail.

4. Mystic-spiritualism

When my second wife and I started dating, I was going through significant changes in my life, namely relationships, work, and home. She told me she had consulted an astrologer many years before to map her astrological birth chart. The results had been revealing. So, on our first dating anniversary, after finding the papers of her consultation, she decided her gift would be my chart, which the same astrologer would do. I contacted him and informed my personal details: full name, date of birth, place and time. Being a much sought-after professional, he told me our appointment would be in two months. Accordingly, I went to his office in the city's southern area on the scheduled day.

As I was in a northern neighbourhood, I had to cross the city and thus face traffic congestion. Consequently, I arrived at the last minute, still agitated. After ringing the bell, I said my name through the intercom, and the door opened to a reception room, where I waited for the astrologer. The atmosphere was charming and relaxing, which brought me peace. There was a subtle scent in the air, an essence of herbs and flowers; in the background, quiet and calming music and the soothing sound of running water nearby. I nearly dozed off while waiting for the astrologer for about 10 minutes. The relaxing effect of the room's tranquil atmosphere certainly acted on my external chaotic pace.

Finally, the astrologer, whose name was Luis, came to meet me and led me to a private room. He invited me to sit in a cosy armchair near his table and offered me a glass of water. After that, he reviewed my personal details to ensure all information was correct before starting to read my map. He then opened a big sheet of paper on the table, where he had drawn it. He also informed me that the session would be recorded and that he would give me all the material afterwards. Finally, the reading started. He began by talking about the planetary conjunction, mentioning the influence of each planet over its sector on the map or the houses: the conjunction of Saturn with Mars retrograde in the ninth house, representing an opportunity in the professional area, potential changes and the opening of new possibilities. Everything followed my expectations for a standard astrological reading.

Sometimes, my mind wandered, but then I noticed that in the middle of some general comments, the astrologer made a few unexpected and specific ones: 'You'll have two children, one very connected to sports, the other will be academic. One of them will probably be a challenge for you, questioning you and your authority as a father.' And then: 'In the fifth house, we see that Pluto brings a positive influence...'

The conversation flowed naturally, exploring the subjects intermittently: in some moments, he spoke of pure astrology, and after a while, he would address premonitions about relationships. 'Saturn at 20 degrees of Capricorn, Mars in the first house brings strength and competitiveness to business. I also see an influence from Jupiter retrograde that opens a window for questioning, a reassessment of relationships...'

But then: 'Your father's grief developed into a severe illness. At the time of their separation, you were very young, and you only heard one side of the story, that of your mother's. Now, it would be essential that you meet him and listen to the other side, that of your father's. That will help you personally in many ways: your compulsion to work and a significant portion of your drive are connected with your constant search for your father.'

Now he was talking about the past, my instinctive thought was, 'enough is enough', and I interrupted the reading.

'One moment, please. How can you possibly know that? Could you show me on the map where you see this? Your comments about my father?'

He looked at me and serenely asked whether I would like to take a break or have some tea, but I refused. Then he inquired if he could proceed and continue reading, avoiding further details or explanations. I agreed and quietly continued listening with no additional questioning. After all, I was the one who looked for him.

'As I mentioned before', he continued, the reconciliation with your father will also help you to work on the issue of your ancestry, on previous relationships. With your father, you will find answers that will help you better raise your future children. Consequently, you will be able to be a better father and, at the same time, break this cycle: your father's relationship with his mother and yours with your children and their children.'

The consultation must have lasted about two hours. I thanked him and went home, trying not to overthink the meeting. I had received a flood of information; consequently, I would need some time to digest it.

Years passed, I married Aline, and we had our first child in 2005. Guilherme was born at 20h20min on 17 February: a healthy big boy weighing 3.5 kg. He was born under the influence of Aquarius, with Libra ascendant. The 'coincidence' was unbelievable: I was born at 10h10min, just like Aline, born on a February morning. She is Aquarius, I am Libra, and Guilherme was born under both signs: Aquarius with Libra ascendant, at 20h20min, the exact sum of his parent's birth times. Coincidences do not exist because I believe in divine providence. Not a single leaf falls from its tree without his consent. Guilherme's birth was paramount to my healing: I had to get well as soon as possible to exercise full paternity.

Two and a half years after that, on 14 August 2007, our second son was born. Ricardo, a Leo, was also a strong and healthy boy, just like Guilherme. Our offspring, our unconditional love. What a joy!

My father's brother, Eliseu, visited us on this occasion. He told me that dad had gone through a tough time between the end of 2005 and early 2006, a problem related to his health, prostate cancer. Despite the hardships, dad considered himself cured.

There was no need for surgery (the fear of doctors was definitely hereditary) or radiotherapy. His only treatment was having a leuprolide injection every three months, a drug that had recently been developed in the USA and was supposed to cure the disease. At that moment, he was already leading an everyday life, and everything was fine.

I decided the time to see my father again had come, and, in my mind, I needed to find an excuse to go to Miami and visit him. The solution was to inform a made-up business trip, hence the reservation with Sofitel at the Blue Lagoon Miami, a hotel close to the airport and near dad's house. Uncle Eliseu decided to accompany me, as did my cousin Eduardo, who was living in Brazil but had to travel regularly to the USA because of his green card.

I would finally meet my father again! When we departed at the end of November, I had butterflies in my stomach. It was a mixture of anxiety and apprehension because the last time I had seen him was for a moment in August 2000. On that occasion, I was embarking on a cruise departing from Miami, so I had some time in the city. We met at a café and had a short chat, less than twenty minutes long. It was undoubtedly worse for my uncle, as he had last met his brother eighteen years before.

We left the airport and parked in front of his house's garage. What a moving reunion! We barely had time to open the car's doors when the two brothers ran towards each other for the most awaited hug in a long time in their lives. That long hug cut deep into my soul: my uncle kept his hand on my dad's neck, who in turn was holding his brother's back and shoulder firmly, with the strength of someone facing a cyclone, the emotional storm of the presence of absence. What a tight hug!

We felt the contagious energy coming from them, filling us with emotion. It was as if we were watching the film of our lives in a few seconds. I went back to my childhood, to my family's story that was interrupted so many years ago. I ran to my father and gave him my tightest hug. We were living a long-awaited dream, loaded with profound sentiments.

Those days we spent together were remarkable. We exchanged information and news about the whole family. Ziza (my uncle's childhood nickname) had to supply detailed information to his eager brother on their life choices, present situation, who married who, who had graduated or given up their studies. Not surprisingly, dad wanted to fill in the blanks of his own life with stories of the family he had left so many years ago, as if it were an album of pictures, with missing photos and faces that had changed over time.

Later on, during lunchtime, dad gave a speech about our family and how important it was for him to have us in his home. At this point, I remember speaking about my feelings of being incomplete because of his absence and also how much I missed him. Furthermore, I mentioned that since separation and his second marriage, our gatherings had gone from weekends and whole holidays together to sporadic dinners at his house, which, because of so much formality, caused a gradual detachment between us.

For the time being, the mood changed. We had had enough emotional declarations for our first reunion, so we decided to make up for lost time and enjoy one another's company. Going deeper into reasons for past events or opening our hearts about them could wait till the next meeting.

After our return to Brazil, dad sent an e-mail to uncle Eliseu in which he expressed his feelings about our reunion:

"Back to the subject of our meeting after so many years, I believe it was the work of God. Don't you think so? I have been praying lately for a chance to be with you again because it seemed that a part of me was missing, and that disturbed me. And then, Glory to God, my prayers were answered because I'm absolutely sure that you also felt a missing part. To me, Eugenia hasn't changed at all: the same face, she looks younger! You too, Ziza, the same Eliseu. Sure, the years have passed, but you've kept your features and still look like my dear brother, the same from our childhood and youth. It was so good to be with you because, in my heart, I believe we've never been apart!'

A few months after our return to Brazil, Ricardo still a baby in my arms, I was invited to manage a hotel in Santa Fe, Mexico City. So, we left for our new destination in January 2009.

It was July of that same year when I got a call from my stepmother asking me to go to Miami as soon as possible. Unfortunately, my father's health had deteriorated because of the cancer relapse, and she feared there would not be much time before his departure. Following our speaking, I immediately contacted my director and explained that we needed to leave for Miami in haste. I then requested our passports, which were at the Immigration Office for visa regularisation.

He explained that the migration process in Mexico was very bureaucratic: if we collected our passports before it was completed, we would be back to square one. Therefore, he asked me to consider waiting a few weeks, as the visas should have been granted by then.

Those days dragged on very slowly for our family. My stepmother called weekly to keep us informed: dad was at homecare, and his only medicine was strong painkillers as palliative treatment. She believed he was just waiting for our arrival to pass away. It was already mid-August when, at long last, the company's lawyer informed me we could get our passports. We flew to Miami on 21 August 2009, a three-hour flight from Mexico City, and went straight to the Sofitel Blue Lagoon.

When we arrived at dad's house, I was shocked by his appearance and the deterioration of his body. His countenance had utterly changed since the last time I saw him. He had lost a lot of weight, but his eyes shone with our presence, in striking contrast to the paleness of his forehead, pale yellowish complexion, and prominent ears, all framed by thinning hair. He made a point of welcoming us at the sitting room door wearing blue pyjamas, slippers and his broad smile. For most of his life, he had been a journalist and communicator and had always taken good care of his teeth. After all, his mouth, with an ever-present contagious smile, was his instrument of communication. He was instantly fascinated by the children, his grandchildren, whom he finally met. He found the strength to play with the boys and talk with us; even from his bed, he never took his eyes off the kids. Being attentive to whatever they did was his way to enjoy every second of that long-awaited connection.

'Look at Ricardo, how smart he is, what fast thinking he has,' he said. 'And Guilherme, intelligent, can talk about anything. I'm impressed with these boys!' He was pure joy. Most of the time, he was lying on his bed, in the room next to the sitting room, specially prepared for him, with all the necessary equipment for palliative support and comfort. Finally, after a few hours, we returned to the hotel, so my father could rest. It had been a hectic day for all of us.

The next day, he sat at the table with us for lunch. He tried to eat a bit of the meat broth but gave up after two spoonfuls.

Despite all his effort not to show it, Dad was in pain. Nevertheless, our presence brought enjoyment to his life, and he wanted to delight in every moment of that pleasant experience.

At dusk, my stepmother, and Aline decided to go shopping and took the boys with them. Consequently, my father and I were alone in the house. We were in his bedroom when I decided to touch the pending matter and tell him the whole story.

'Dad, when I came here with uncle Eliseu two years ago, I told you I had a business meeting. But the truth is, that was only an excuse. I wanted to see you because of something I learnt some years ago before the boys were born. I had a consultation with an astrologer who read my birth chart. He undoubtedly has mystical abilities because, while reading the map, something intriguing happened: he stopped citing the stars' influence and mentioned your illness. He said grief had triggered it, and I should hear your side of the story, as I'd only heard Mum's. Doing so would help our relationship. He also said that my unchecked compulsion to work developed because I kept looking for you in my professional activities. Finally, he advised that I listen to you, which would help us both and would be fundamental in my future life as a father. We would work together for change, something like breaking an ancestral, karmic cycle.'

My father looked at me, deeply into my eyes. He then asked me to bring a chair next to his bed and sit on it.

'I don't know the person who told you this, but he's certainly a wise man', he said. He went on, saying that he hadn't been a good father to me, that after the separation, he had been unable to reconcile our relationship with that of his new family's. 'I love you both so much', he added, 'I'd give a piece of me for your sister

70

or you; I've suffered a lot, and I regret it.' I replied that I loved him unconditionally and had kept the happy moments with him and his teachings from my childhood. He had been an example to me: I never heard him raise his voice to my mother, and he was a worthy man, one of great honour. Besides, he had been the best father in the world, and I also felt sorry our relationship had been brief.

'Do you know what happened to my mother?' he asked. 'One day, I came home from school and found a note from her. She had left home and abandoned us, my younger brother, my father and me. So that day, I told my brother to stay home and went looking for her. Imagine the drama: a lonely boy, perplexed by the situation, wandering the streets and trying to find his mom. I found her eventually, in an immodest place, and begged her to come home with me, but she never did.' And he completed: 'We went on with our lives, me trying to take care of my younger brother, my father absolutely disconsolate. We were all broken-hearted.'

Our conversation took place on 22 August, and we returned to Mexico the following morning; life followed the routine in the new country. It was already September, and I woke up on a Thursday feeling good. That night, I dreamed of my father. It was a dinner scene: there were several people at a long table, and my father was standing by it. He was talking to everyone with his genuine, contagious smile, his figure no longer the one from some days ago, fragile and sick, but as I remembered him, younger, with long and wavy hair, elegant and displaying his exuberant charisma. In my dream, I said:

'Dad, you look amazing! Was it the new treatment?'

He looked at me and said: 'Yes, I'm very well, entirely recovered.' He smiled and left.

71

I shared my dream with my wife and went to work. A few hours later, I was still at the hotel, and my phone rang. It was Aline informing me that my father had died. Thursday, 10 September 2009: the same day as my dream.

Conclusions

This diary's objective is to increase awareness of mental health problems. I hope to help this by making public my psychotic breakdown that started on 29 April 2004 and its healing process. Furthermore, may it serve as a reference for people going through the same hardships, and may my testimony support them in overcoming their crises. Believe me, writing about my breakdown was no easy task; it was exhausting, lonely and emotional work. On top of that, I have learnt that mental health issues should not be treated as a taboo: statistics show that one in four people will present some of them during their lives.

The Covid-19 pandemic had devastating impacts on the mental health of the world's population: it increased the risk of a parallel pandemic, escalating psychological suffering, psychic symptoms and mental disorders, all intensified by social distancing.

When going through traumatic experiences like this one, we often think, 'it's difficult, but I'll get over it. I don't need help, and I'll recover soon. It'll pass.' However, we do not realise, not even with the physical signals sent by our bodies, that these events leave deep psychological marks, like wounds in the soul, hurting the unconscious. Equally important, we do not acknowledge that they accumulate like flooded water, which causes the breaking of barriers and severe consequences for our psychic functions and social relationships.

We live in a fast-paced society. It is consumerist, ruthless, and full of passion and excess, which creates unhealthy conditions for its members, frequently transmissible through heredity and inherent to our material world.

In critical situations, when we repeatedly disrespect our body's limits, we are unconsciously turned off by nature through our conservation instinct. In other words, providence takes over, making us temporarily spectators of our fate. It is a necessary intervention to avoid more significant danger, as well as to restore our physical, psychic and spiritual balance, and so move on with our lives. A relevant aspect linked to this act is the feeling of impotence when facing reality: the individual loses control of their faculties. Therefore, we must resign ourselves to suffering the consequences of the environment in which our inferiority places us. In the healing process, medical intervention becomes critical, and so does the unconditional support of family and friends in moral, psychological, philosophical and spiritual support.

I am grateful for the breakdown because it has made me a better human being. Nowadays, I pay more attention to the signals my body sends: lack of sleep, for example, immediately transmits warning alerts to my soul, fearful of committing the same faults. I also do my best to be more tolerant of others, since aggressive words are like poison darts that affect their heart and possibly their mental health. Above all, I thank God for my healing, and I pray for those who lived through the same experience and did not have the same luck and protection.

The journey has been long but enriching. I followed my treatment in the three ways I mentioned before: medication (antipsychotics, antidepressants and natural remedies); change of habits, including diet, a lot of reading and quality time; analysis of past events and a path to self-knowledge. Consequently,

I could understand the triggers and reasons that culminated in my illness, and I have learnt to be alert so that it does not return.

I am also grateful for the doors that opened due to the crisis. The reunion with my father and my faith restoration established a solid foundation. In addition, the exceptional protection I had throughout the event when I was freaking out and alone for days on end, exposed to the most varied risks during great mental confusion and delusion, testifies that my guardian angel watched over me. Last but not least, I am grateful for the publication of this diary.

There were also messages sent by divine providence during my journey that, I confess, went unnoticed or sometimes plainly ignored. That happened because I was absent from the present, immersed in anxiety about future events that might not happen. However, my faith was revitalised: 'seek your father', said that wise, inspired astrologer. That recommendation has given us much. In other words, it was a vital part of my healing and served as a balm for the departure of dad's physical being. He left comforted but not without paying me a farewell visit in my dream on 10 September 2009, the date of his death and, not by chance, the eve of 11 September.

More than two decades later, the memories of the attack live in my soul. The aftermath of this ruthless war still unfolds even now: we have welcomed Afghan refugees to hotels in Wales, where I live and work nowadays. They are souls who leave everything behind, even their own family, and remain outcasts wandering the world, victims of their destiny. They are not responsible for the attacks, so I receive them with solidarity. I try to accept the facts because I know that nothing happens by chance, which is why I have recorded everything in this diary.

TESTIMONIES

Aline Gonzaga Moreira – Wife

Douglas has always been a dedicated professional and passionate about what he does. More than that, he invariably invests all his energy in projects in every hotel he has worked for. Endowed with a restless, impatient and insightful nature, Douglas has routinely looked for new challenges, pushing his limits and strength to achieve his goals. One of them was to have an international career, which demanded spotless professional performance and agility to overcome obstacles. So, in early 2003, Douglas moved to the country in São Paulo to manage a hotel from the economic brand of an international company as part of a strategy to pursue his career. He would return to São Paulo during the weekends, or I would visit him.

Everything was going as planned until, in late 2003, he lost Whiskey, his beloved dog. They were walking around the building's shared area, where Douglas was living, when a car came from nowhere and ran over the little animal. The driver did not stop to help but ran away.

It was late afternoon in midweek, so Douglas was alone in town. In a state of shock, feeling immense pain and holding Whiskey in his arms, he did not know what to do. The loss shook him to the core, and over time the absence of family and friends during the week left him discouraged and saddened. That was when I had a 'brilliant' idea of getting another dog to keep him company. But Meg, a beautiful and excessively energetic beagle, did not give Douglas a minute's rest. She was so excitable that on one occasion, she tried to chew the cord of an electrical appliance in the kitchen and lost a part of her mouth and tongue – another trauma for Douglas.

On that weekend in May 2004, Douglas would be back in São Paulo on Friday night as usual. However, upon his arrival, I could see he was very agitated, talking in detail about the meeting he attended during the week in Santo André. Douglas then told me how hard driving back was because the headlights of cars in the opposite direction were too bright, so he could not see well and felt it difficult to concentrate. He also thought he was being watched, an unusual comment, but I did not worry about it then. It had been a tiring and busy week, and we were about to leave for our nephew Eric's birthday party, to which we arrived late.

I got home around half past one in the morning and went straight to bed. At 3 am, Douglas called my mobile and told me to take some notes, to write down a list, because there were things he could not forget. I was confused, not completely awake, and could not understand what was happening. It felt like a dream; he kept talking, no pause: 'Write it down, we're going to travel, so get your passport. I've uncovered a scheme, some employees are stealing money from the company, and they know I know and will come after me. I can't stand still!' And then he ended the call.

That disturbed me, for it did not make sense at all. We had just met, but Douglas did not say anything. Was he talking during sleep? Having somnambulism episodes now? I could not sleep anymore, and at 5 am, he called again, saying he could not speak, asking me to meet him and repeating similar instructions: 'Write everything for me on the list, get your passport, we're going away, I need to get out of here.' Again, he would not let me talk and kept speaking until hanging up again.

The second call worried me even more. It was anything but ordinary: not a dream again, let alone somnambulism! I went to my parents' room. My father was awake, so I said: 'Dad, I'm very concerned about Douglas. He is not well. He called me twice during the night and had a frantic tone in his voice. Not only that, but he also said he couldn't sleep and mentioned absurd things, some paranoid ideas. I thought he was dreaming or sleep-walking, but the same words twice are not normal. I'm worried!'

My father sat up and said: 'He must be having a psychotic breakdown. We need to call his mother at once and ask them to take him to a hospital.' 'Why do you think that?' I asked. He replied, 'A person close to me went through a comparable situation a few years ago. Douglas's probably had some sleepless nights already, which can become a paranoid cycle, so he needs urgent assistance. We must proceed immediately: call your mother-in-law and tell her what is happening.'

At 6 am, I went to my sister-in-law Glaucia's house to stay with Douglas. Shortly after that, his mother, Deise, arrived with Abilio, her partner. I told them everything that had happened, including my father's comments. We were all perplexed: no one understood what was going on or knew how to act. After we talked to him, Douglas agreed to go to his mother's house, and I accompanied him.

Later, after lunch, he seemed more conscious and invited me for a car ride. We were on Gabriel Monteiro da Silva Avenue when Douglas asked me to stop at the car park of a classy chandelier shop. Looking around very suspiciously, he decided to go into the store. After being enquired, the shop assistant informed us the door in the middle of the room was the lift to the upper floor, and she invited us to see it.

Douglas refused and said we should leave the shop. His behaviour became unusual again; every movement and word seemed strategically premeditated, his speech was more paused, and everything was weird.

While I was driving back to Deise's house, Douglas told me he thought people were following him, which was why we stopped at the shop. When the shop assistant showed the lift in the middle of the hall, he was sure they would abduct him if we got into it.

I felt a chill down my spine, my thoughts were racing, and I could not believe what I was hearing. It seemed surreal! 'God, what's happening?' I thought. He seemed better, but he was not well at all! I was sure we needed help urgently. But what should we do? Would he stay like that forever? What despair!

We arrived at his mother's house, and Douglas went to the TV room, locking himself in with Meg, the dog, to supposedly protect him. He asked me to leave at some point because he had discovered that I was part of the plot and that the scheme was much bigger than he had imagined. I was embezzling the company's money with the help of the HR manager! Negotiations followed for hours at the room door: Douglas inside, opening and closing the door with every word he said; Deise, Abilio and I, trying to understand and calm him down. It was very exhausting and distressing for us. Eventually, Deise asked me to go home and rest, as I had not slept well. I agreed and left, but I called her often to follow up on the situation.

Douglas was still locked in the TV room, in a state of paranoia, as he described in his diary. He could not sleep. His mind would not disconnect; everything was bizarre, and our energy was already drained.

On Sunday morning, things reached a critical point. Deise and Abilio took him to the hospital, and she sent me a message, which I saw after waking up. When I arrived, Douglas was in the ward, lying down but ordering the place, telling the staff to collect the rubbish from the dustbins and to sweep the floor. He had a suspicious look out of the corner of his eye, as if apprehensive. Despite that, he asked me to approach him and said everything was fine and under control, adding that he would talk to the psychiatrist soon and the doctor would discharge him.

And he was right: Douglas was discharged after twenty minutes of talking with the psychiatrist! When we left the hospital, he asked me to drive him and, during the ride, told me that he had not swallowed the pill, that he had hidden it under his tongue and later thrown it in a potted plant because he feared the doctor would make him stay in the hospital forever. Moreover, Douglas tried to convince him everything was fine and that he only needed to rest from a stressful period.

I panicked! If he had convinced a psychiatrist he was not ill, then he would undoubtedly do the same with other doctors. What now?

Upon arriving at Deise's home, Douglas proceeded to lock himself again, and I told everyone he had not swallowed the medication. His cousin Maria Lucia, whom we call Malu, a psychologist, came to our help. However, after conversing with Douglas, she stated that there was no other solution: hospitalisation was the best measure for him. So Glaucia swung into action, starting with a phone call to the company's HR manager. At 5 pm, the ambulance arrived with three nurses, one of whom was a huge man. Douglas tried to negotiate with them by opening the door no more than a gap. Eventually, one of the nurses managed to put his foot in the door, so Douglas could not close it. Now he had no way out.

Malu convinced him to have an injection with a strong sedative. Subsequently, the nurses took him to the clinic. A few days later, he told me about another hallucination while inside the ambulance: they were taking him to a gas chamber after the Twin Towers were hit!

It all felt like a never-ending nightmare. Meanwhile, Deise and I drove to the clinic, where we met the person in charge of human relations, a saint who helped us with the hospitalisation process following the company's health insurance policy.

We saw hurting scenes of other patients arriving at the clinic while we waited in the reception area. Douglas' head was on my lap, sleeping like an angel, and we were downhearted for not knowing what would come subsequently. After getting home, I burst into tears as I could not believe the surrounding events were real. Three apprehensive days followed; he was sleeping when I visited him, so we could not talk to each other.

On discharge day, we spoke to the doctor responsible; her evaluation report was a relief. Considering Douglas' age, 34 years old, she believed he had had an isolated psychotic episode triggered by stress. She said it was unlikely to happen again, but emphasised the importance of continued medical monitoring, particularly controlling pressure through a good night of sleep. If, by any chance, he had any sleep deprivation, it would be essential to relax through leisure activities and burn energy with exercises. Controlling the quality of his sleep became vital to Douglas' rehabilitation.

The doctor also explained clearly how the brain works. The neurons have the primary function of conducting nerve impulses and the ability to establish connections with each other when receiving stimuli from the external environment or from the body itself. When a psychotic breakdown happens, the neurons stop establishing this connection, hence mental confusion, hallucinations, disorganised or incoherent speech, mood swings, and loss of time perception, among other symptoms.

Consequently, a sleep treatment is like a reboot of the neurological system. But, to reassure us, the doctor also mentioned that the number of breakdown cases among company executives was increasing yearly and that Douglas' was far from being a unique case.

After his psychotic breakdown, Douglas felt fragile: he was afraid it could happen again, and his fear haunted his thoughts night and day, leaving him permanently alert. At that moment, he needed our love, support, patience, and understanding because it is not a situation one recovers from in a few days. Instead, it is a long healing journey that takes months, sometimes even years.

His company supported him throughout the process, particularly his friend in the HR department and his boss. Their understanding was fundamental for his gradual return to work. Still, it was not easy for Douglas: his days had become grey, and his joie de vivre was only a shadow.

In July, we went on holiday to Recife and Fernando de Noronha[15]. Douglas' recovery process was still ongoing, which meant that he had some relapses. Some things he would say during these occasions left me apprehensive or suspicious. I wondered whether he would heal completely, and I hoped for it.

---

15. TN – Recife is a coastal city on the Northeast coast of Brazil. Fernando de Noronha is a volcanic archipelago about 540 kilometres from Recife; it is a marine protected area and ecological sanctuary,

Moreover, he still had not been discharged: that would happen only a year later.

With the arrival of our son Guilherme in February 2005, Douglas returned to work. He had committed himself to learning how to control his stress on a daily basis, and his efforts paid off because he was soon transferred to São Paulo. The new job helped his recovery immensely; after all, he was close to his family and friends. Moreover, after the birth of Ricardo, our second son, Douglas could focus on his international career, which had been his dream for a long time.

The breakdown was not an obstacle to his professional improvement, but rather a lesson on how to moderate his lifestyle: he learnt how to control his working hours and to practise physical activities to balance his emotional exhaustion.

Today, 18 years after the episode, Douglas decided to open his heart, to share everything he experienced, to help other patients and their family members who are going through the same situation, to show the path to his personal healing and, mostly, that it is possible to overcome such challenging difficulties and adversity.

As a girlfriend at that time and a wife today, I would like to give a few words of advice to family members going through a tough time. During a psychotic breakdown, the patient loses touch with reality, so it is essential to avoid confrontation. It is important to treat the person with comprehension, empathy, and calm and never to react harshly, as the breakdown creates a lot of emotional instability. The patient's delusions and hallucinations are real to them. Therefore, it is no use trying to persuade them otherwise, either by contradicting or showing facts. It is of utmost importance to have a person present to defuse the situation, prevent the patient from harming themselves, and immediately seek professional medical help. The most critical alert factors for family members to recognise a psychotic breakdown are disorganised or incoherent thinking and speaking, mental confusion, agitated behaviour, irritability, mood swings and changes in the sleep cycle.

Today, looking back, I see how vital the support of both his family and employers was during the entire healing process. I remember they sent Douglas a beautiful breakfast basket when he left the clinic, which touched him enormously.

Glaucia Gonçalves – Sister

I can say it was not an easy experience. As in a dream, or rather a nightmare, I actively took part in this 'tropical delirium'. I must confess that, in the beginning, it was difficult to identify what was happening. Besides escalating gradually, it concerned a person I loved, someone remarkably close to me and above any suspicion: my brother.

It was late Thursday night, and I politely listened to how the management meeting in Santo André had gone. He was all enthusiasm, attentive gaze, much gesticulating, restless and expressive as ever. The only difference I noticed was that, since Mother's Day[16] on the previous weekend, he had been vehemently demanding attention from his audience.

During that night, which was my son's fifth birthday, I also noticed a kind of overstatement in his remarks, for example, when he said he was sure the meeting had been held especially for him.

'How could a meeting of managers from all over Brazil have been held exclusively for him?' I thought.

---

16. TN – In Brazil, Mother's Day is celebrated on the second Sunday of May.

It was already a signal that something was wrong, but I did not give much thought to it, just telling him I thought he was exaggerating. We were up all night talking, and Douglas told me more stories about what had happened during the days of the meeting. He mentioned the speech and the round of applause he got, the issue with the safe's password, how the room had been cleaned, the towel left on purpose in a strategic place and, finally, his suspicion that he was being constantly observed and evaluated.

Although I found this a little odd, I did not give it much thought. In other words, I did not realise how absurd it was. Finally, at 3:30 am, I went to sleep. It was almost 5 am when I heard my brother's footsteps towards the kitchen. 'Probably having some water', I thought, but then I noticed the TV in his room was still on. I wondered if he had not been able to sleep. However, we would celebrate my little one's birthday the next day, so I let it go.

The party would start at 8 pm; he arrived at a quarter past 7. I was getting ready to leave the house when he took me aside, said he was not feeling well and added, anxiously, he believed himself to be the victim of a plot. His words left me bewildered, and I did not know what to do. I could not and did not want to leave him alone, but I needed to go to be at the party's place when the guests arrived. Luckily, our mother came at that moment, so I left them talking and went to my room to get my handbag. After that, we asked him to go to the spiritist centre near my house to take fluid therapy; besides, I said I would come back to pick him up.

About half an hour before the party ended, Douglas arrived with his girlfriend, and I felt relieved: he looked well. We left around 11 pm; my son started coughing a bit later. I gave him a spoonful of syrup and tucked him into bed. Mom and Douglas' girlfriend went talking with him until 1:30 am. Then, as I was exhausted, I decided to sleep; basically, everything seemed fine.

Soon after that, my son started coughing again. I got up several times and gave him more syrup, and later, a bit of honey with lemon juice, but nothing would stop the cough. That is when I decided to take him to casualty. I asked Douglas to pull his car away from the driveway and told him I would call with the news. Then, as I would not be back soon, I made the bed and left.

After my son was medicated, I called my brother to inform him that it was nothing serious and that we would soon be back home. It was 4 am when we returned, and I did not find Douglas in the house. Where would he have gone at that hour? I put my sleeping son in his bed and went to the room where my brother was sleeping to look for clues. I was alarmed to find a Batman's action figure in the hallway, another on top of a piece of furniture in the living room, and one more on my bed. The last one was inside the gifts' bag from the party with a note in which I identified Douglas' handwriting: 'Thank you'. That was when it hit me: 'My brother is not well at all! What the heck does this mean?' Would Douglas be on drugs? If yes, it could be cocaine because he had not slept in two days. I was distraught, imagining where he could be because he had taken the car.

What now? What should I do? I thought of calling our mother, but decided against it, as it would only make her even more worried. I decided to wait a little longer and, lo and behold, he arrived and went straight to the kitchen. Immediately, I heard the noise of cabinet doors opening and closing and decided to check what Douglas was doing. To my surprise, he was putting away the items from the food parcel he always brought us. It was unusual, as my brother had never taken such an initiative. I asked if everything was alright, and the answer was yes. Then he asked if his nephew had improved; I replied and inquired where he had gone at that time in the morning. Douglas hesitated a bit and then said he had gone to the pharmacy to buy sore throat tablets. The answer did not convince me, but I decided not to question it for the time being. I said good night and finally went to bed.

It was almost 5 am when I woke up with a phone call. Still disoriented, I found my mobile inside my handbag, and, to my astonishment, it was a call from my own house. I heard my brother's voice calling my number from the room he was: 'Hello. Please, put another name on the list.'

'What?' I replied, 'what list? It's your sister, Douglas! What do you want?'

'Oh, is that you? I'm sorry. Do you have Aline's phone number?'

That is when I lost patience and replied furiously.

'Why do you want her number now? Do you know what time it is? 5 am! Go to sleep, please!'

I was very sleepy; however, my concern for his condition was greater, so I decided to stay awake and vigilant. It was almost 6 am when I heard the front door slam: Aline had come at his request. When I left, the door of his bedroom was still closed. I spoke to her later, and she was sure he was having a breakdown. She said that we needed to take him to a doctor as soon as possible because the same thing had happened to an aunt of hers, and she warned me that the longer we allowed him to go undiagnosed, the worse it would get.

What? Where shall we take him? Which hospital? I had no idea about his health insurance plan. Now what? What had caused this? What could have triggered this problem?

I wondered about the meeting. Had something more serious happened there that he did not tell me? Or maybe something in the hotel he managed, something disturbing? Could I really trust everything he had told me? What had been real, and what was his imagination? Although there was a logical sequence of ideas and thoughts, I was baffled, not knowing what we could think of it.

I made a mental retrospective of everything that had happened until I got to 9 May, a Sunday, when we had our Mother's Day lunch. Douglas said we should go to a famous Italian restaurant in the Jardins neighbourhood.

I recalled he had not stopped talking throughout the whole lunch. He spoke essentially to himself about his work, his enthusiasm for the neurolinguistic classes, the French teacher, his willingness to change his behaviour, and his expectations at the hotel. I thought he was somewhat artificial, as if he were acting. Still, my assessment was interrupted (and even forgotten) when Douglas suddenly asked me, in a way that showed he knew the answer:

'Do you find me different?'

'Yes, a little', I replied.

'It's because I'm checking my gestures', he said and pointed at his index finger. 'This, in neurolinguistic, denotes aggressiveness.' But, my brother continued, he was already working on it, as we could see.

Nevertheless, I needed more details about that past week and wondered who could tell me what had happened during the meeting. That was when our dear friend who worked at the company's HR came to mind. She had taken part in the meeting, but most importantly, I knew my brother trusted her. So, I found her phone number among his things and called her. Very carefully, I made inquiries about her impressions of my brother during the meeting. She told me that she actually found him a little fragile, emotionally speaking, and tense. She confirmed the stories he had told me (which comforted me a lot), including the one about the speech, which started a bit weirdly but then improved and finished up very well, drawing applause from those present. Phew! At least professionally, he is alright, I thought, relieved.

If he was having a breakdown, as Aline suspected, we needed to get him to a hospital as soon as possible to be treated, but how? He would not agree to it and did not want to go at all. I was already losing my little patience because he insisted that we hear his fantastic stories, and the more we questioned him or showed interest, the more he talked and lengthened them and kept talking.

That was when I was sure we were not helping him at all. Quite the contrary, we were only setting him off, so he continued daydreaming. Therefore, I decided to be more assertive and harshly said he needed medical help, which started an argument.

Behold, the bell rang! It was Abilio who, facing the unhinged situation, asked us to calm down and bring him 'The Gospel according to Spiritualism', a book by Allan Kardec so that we could pray. As soon as Abilio started reading, Douglas cried, hugged our mother and asked to go to her house, to which she promptly agreed.

That night, I slept soundly; after all, my brother was safe at our mother's house. But was he sound?

Sunday, 9:30 am: the phone rings. It was my cousin Malu asking how Douglas was.

'Not so good', I replied, 'why?'

'Because he called me in the middle of the night', she said, 'about 3 am, saying he needed to talk to me, that I was his therapist. Then aunt Deise got on the phone and said they were taking him to the hospital. A moment later, he called again, asking if I could come along, and our aunt stepped in again, saying it wasn't necessary. She confirmed he wasn't alright and added they would call me later with the news.'

Oh God, I thought, what was going on with him? For the time being, I could not join them, because it was street market day, and I could not take the car. So, I just assumed that everything was under control – a big mistake.

Around noon, I decided to call my mother, and with a tense voice, she said: 'You need to come here right now. We need to talk.'

Upon arriving at mom's house, she told me Douglas had locked himself in the TV room and that having a conversation with him was impossible. He had already kicked Aline out, taken the dog hostage to act as a guard at the door and, consequently, kept mom with him. What a scene! At least mom had already confiscated all the keys to the flat's doors.

She told me that he had not let them sleep, asking them to read a page of the Gospel and pray with him all the time. Finally, at 3 am, Abilio decided enough was enough and demanded that Douglas go with them to the hospital. When they arrived at Nove de Julho Hospital, the nurse checked his blood pressure, which was remarkably high! He was medicated by the general practitioner and then referred to the on-call psychiatrist, so they sent him a message. Finally, he arrived after making us wait for about four hours. He chatted a little, prescribed a pill that Douglas spat out as soon as no one was looking at him, and discharged my brother after twenty minutes. Mind you: I said twenty minutes.

I am a layperson, but that has not kept me from disapproving of this doctor's procedure. At the very least, I found it insensitive to someone who was visibly in the middle of a breakdown, considering that he had not shown any improvement while in the hospital. Furthermore, how could he discharge Douglas so quickly without keeping him under observation for longer? In fact, I not only judged this doctor, but indeed condemned him for such an attitude.

Back at our mother's flat, where Douglas locked himself again, I tried to talk to him, with no result. After the formal, 'please, open the door', I had to identify myself. He cracked the door open and looked at me with an indignant face. I asked to be allowed in, to which my brother responded by giving me a little more space, but at the same time, standing in front of me to prevent any advance. All I could do was ask if he was okay, and he said yes. He added he could not talk to me and that I smelled awfully. Next, he pushed me away and locked the door one more time. Wow, the thing was much more serious than I thought. What should we do?

Mom informed us that the hospital psychiatrist had left his contact, just in case, and we decided to call him. If Douglas had not improved with the medicine the doctor gave him – on the contrary, he was worse – I found it difficult to trust a new prescription, but we had no alternative. It was 1 pm when we first left him a message asking him to get in touch.

After fifteen minutes, a second attempt, to which there was no reply. Twenty minutes passed, and nothing came from him. One more message followed, and, finally, near 3 pm, he called us back. I explained the critical situation and, in an already distressed voice, begged him to give his opinion, some advice to help us. He then told me we needed to take him back to the hospital so that he could provide us with the hospitalisation guide to a specialised clinic.

I told him that Douglas refused to leave the room to talk to us, let alone go to the hospital. He offered to come to our place to medicate him; however, he would charge a consultation fee. Faced with the situation we were in, I immediately agreed.

Like Abilio, mum was visibly exhausted, with an air of concern and anxiety. Thinking of sparing her, I said she should go to the kitchen and remain there until the dilemma was solved. Meanwhile, I had an idea.

I remembered Malu, our psychologist cousin. How did I not think of her before? If he asked her for help during a breakdown in the middle of the night, perhaps her presence would be enough to make him better and convince him to go to the hospital. So, I promptly called her; it took her fifteen minutes to come to our help, bringing her two children. We quickly explained the situation, and she followed us to the TV room.

As we expected, Douglas allowed her in, and she stayed there for twenty to thirty minutes, an absolute record! Then, she returned to the kitchen, where we were waiting anxiously, and informed us that he was very unstable. He would definitely need medical treatment.

So, well, what about the doctor? Why was he taking so long to come? He told me he only needed to go to a pharmacy to buy the medicine and would come to meet us. He said he was riding a motorcycle, and I supposed he would arrive within an hour at most, considering it was Sunday. However, more than two hours had passed, and we were still anxiously waiting.

In the meantime, since Douglas would clearly need a clinic, I called Jamile, his friend from the hotel, and asked her to recommend a good one. She returned my call within ten minutes, informing the number of a well-recommended clinic. I had no doubt, after Malu came to the kitchen again, saying her strategy to bring him out of the room was not working. Given the total lack of support from the psychiatrist (whose whereabouts we had no idea), I spoke with my mother, and we decided to call the clinic.

A girl with a soft voice answered my call. When I asked if they could pick him up, she said that, unfortunately, they could not, but she had the phone number of an ambulance service known to them. She added that they had been providing such assistance to the clinic for a long time, so that was what I did: I called them.

Being unsure and afraid of the methods they would use, I asked a few questions and pointed to the fact that he was unstable and refused to leave the room. They comforted me, saying that they knew how to proceed because they had a lot of experience dealing with similar cases. In short, I was assured Douglas would leave without any problems.

Although still a bit suspicious, I accepted the recommendation; after all, something had to be done urgently, the circumstances were terrible, and they were our only option. Meanwhile, Douglas had already put some 'threatening' objects outside the room's door and broken a telephone set, which he believed had been bugged.

I was informing our address to the ambulance service when that psychiatrist called. Luckily for him, Aline was the one to answer the phone, and he told her he was on his way. So, when I finished my call, I sent him a message saying not to bother coming. Fifteen minutes later, around 5 pm, he called back, and this time I answered the phone. I told him I was grateful but that he no longer needed to come since we had already decided to send Douglas to a clinic his employer had referred to us, and that the ambulance was on its way. Next, to my surprise, he informed me that he had a clinic 'where your brother will receive all the care he needs.' I politely dismissed his offer, but he continued with a warning tone in his voice.

'Be careful. The less your brother stays in a clinic, the better for him. You know, some clinics would not be the right ones for his case.' Instead of sounding like a warning, his words caused indignation. At that moment, I was sure his main interest was getting Douglas admitted to his private clinic. All the same, he asked permission to come and help in any way, as he had empathised with my brother. I said it did not matter to me and made it clear that our decision had been made. Douglas would not go with him to his clinic, and that was it. I hoped the ambulance would arrive before him, but that was not what happened.

When the doctor arrived, he apologised for the delay (four hours!) and went ahead to see Douglas, still under Malu's watch. A few minutes later, the ambulance crew arrived. The moment I saw them, I immediately understood the 'convincing technique': three men dressed in white, two of average size, and a third one, a monumental, massive, sturdy man. He was as tall as the door frame, so he bent his head when crossing it. But, aside the shocking impression, I soon realised they were kind beyond question. I asked them to wait for the doctor, who was still inside the room. A little after that, Malu joined us at the doctor's request. A quarter of an hour later, he told us he needed more time to convince Douglas to have an injection with an antipsychotic drug.

Malu then returned to the room. About ten minutes after that, my brother finally agreed to have the injection and go with the nurses to the ambulance. (Sometime later, we found out that Malu was the one who convinced him to have the injection.) Then, I saw him calmly leaving the flat and walking backwards next to the ambulance attendants. At that moment, I praised God: my brother would finally get the help he needed.

I did not go with them to the clinic. Instead, I had to return home, and give my son his medication, a bath, and dinner. So, after helping to clean up the TV room, I drove back to my house.

Much later, around 10 pm, I spoke with my mother, and she told me about the hospitalisation. She had talked to a doctor who comforted her, saying that these cases were becoming more frequent, mainly with executives. Although my brother's case was not severe, he needed medication and rest, but he would be fine. Douglas would stay in an Intensive Care Unit overnight and possibly go to the ward the next day. That was precisely what happened. We went to the clinic to visit him at 2 am. They took us to his room, and we saw him lying down, sleeping.

The nurse told us we could wake him up, but that was unnecessary. It seems he noticed our presence and opened his eyes. His look was gentle, full of sweetness. It was so good to see him again, even though he was a little sleepy from the effects of the medication. He told us about the clinic, the people who had treated him very well and the food that he said was delicious.

Personally, I found the place too plain. There were three low, dark wood beds with shabby mattresses. There were no wardrobes, only wooden boxes nailed to the wall for the patients to store their clothes and personal items. I noticed that my brother's box was smaller than the other two, which were already insufficient. They measured about one square metre with a shelf in the middle. The floor was tiled, and the only window, in front of Douglas' bed, was barred. There was nothing else in the room. The door led to a corridor; opposite the room, there was a shared bathroom.

I felt a strange feeling, a certain anxiety, for believing that would not be the right clinic for him, but then I considered that a comfortable and fancy place did not necessarily equate with efficiency. This thought comforted me; in the end, what mattered most was how well he was being treated.

My considerations were interrupted when Douglas said he wanted to shower and put on clean clothes mom had brought. So, we waited, and when he returned, he invited us to visit the clinic. First, my brother showed us the TV room, the swimming pool, the kitchen, the women's section, and the cafeteria. Moreover, he insisted we see the backyard, with some trees, including a jabuticaba and a bougainvillaea. Next, Douglas introduced us to two friends he had already made.

Around 3 pm, we were interrupted by the nurse informing us that visiting hours were over. My brother was a bit perturbed, and so were we, until he made a move and said he would go with us to the gate. Before we could say goodbye, we saw the cafeteria, with a basket of bread and thermos bottles on the table. Douglas asked if we wanted coffee, but the nurse was watching us. So, we thanked him and said we had to go.

And then came one of the hardest moments I had ever been through in my entire life. The feeling I had when I hugged him to say goodbye: in a few seconds, all the memories of the last few days came to my mind like a fast-forwarding film. There was a mixture of sadness and guilt in my soul because I felt personally responsible for his admission into the clinic. Although rationally I knew we had made the right decision, at that moment, I was assaulted by doubt: had the hospitalisation been absolutely necessary? I got in the car, holding back the tears that my mother could not repress. We remained speechless for several minutes, trying to digest everything.

I left my mother at home and went back to work. Along the drive, my head kept spinning in a jumble of feelings. On the one hand, I was happy to see that my brother was recovering well, for he remembered everything that had happened. On the other hand, I felt awful for thinking I could have somehow prevented him from experiencing such intense events, parts of a cruel reality we created as the imperfect beings and poor mortals we are.

To finish my account of those days, I want to share some aspects – if not lessons – of our experience. They have created lasting impressions on my life, deserving of reflection.

*Sense of paralysis in the face of reality. I was with my brother most of the time, with my heart and soul, and still, there was nothing I could do to help him, as he did not even listen to me. Fact: things happen independently of us.

Patience an♦ resignation!

*Unconditional support from our loved ones, our friends, friendly spirits, faithful companions along our evolution, angels sharing our path, always ready to help us, listen patiently, share one another's burdens, make them lighter, and comfort our hearts.

Compassion!

*Spiritual support. Religiosity. The divine presence, constantly perceived, worked as a comforting balm. The most profound conviction that it was a temporary state and that my brother would get well soon overcame the prejudice and helped us keep the greater spirituality channel open.

Faith!

*Expand our scope of action and donation to its maximum; avoid channelling energy into only one or two aspects of our lives: family, personal, professional, or spiritual.

Balance!

*Enjoying our own company, loving ourselves; being less critical, less stubborn and more understanding of ourselves; discovering our limits and learning to respect them.

Self-knowlege!

*Being more tolerant, patient and generous, especially with those around us, the ones we live with, our co-workers, parents, children, siblings, and relatives. Avoid complaining so much: criticise less and love more.

Altruism!

And finally:

*Understanding that nothing comes about by chance and that everything happens for a reason. Joy and gratitude, for I know my brother is healthier than ever and willing to help others, giving what is best in him for those who have not been so lucky.

Provience!

Maria Lucia Oliveri - Psychologist/cousin Malu

It was Sunday afternoon. My children, grandchildren and I had just arrived at the Vila Pompeia May Festival. I got a call asking me to go to my dear Deise's house because my cousin Douglas was not well and wanted to see me. My son Daniel and I did not hesitate.

Upon arriving, we learnt he was locked in the TV room, and I would be the only one he would allow to see him. Daniel stared wide-eyed at me and asked if I felt okay going in alone. Before entering the room, I asked the spiritual mentors to help me find the right words to help Douglas. Our family's religious foundation is the Spiritist Doctrine. 'I am not alone; they will be with me', I replied to my son.

The room resembled a war scenography. Various superheroes and soldiers were arrayed in positions to defend my cousin's 'territory'. I soon realised he was having a breakdown. Stress can trigger an emotional surge. It sets when psychic suffering is acute: the person cannot deal with the crisis resulting from the inability to eliminate day-to-day tensions naturally.

Internal factors, such as individual results, and dissatisfaction with life or oneself, cause emotional stress. However, it can also be triggered by external factors, namely health problems in the family or with friends, traffic, queues, hectic routine, overworking and a highly competitive environment.

Douglas was going through several personal and professional circumstances that led to this lack of control. He paced around the room and talked frantically. Calmly, I asked him to sit down, so we could speak. My cousin began to describe everything he was feeling, including his suspicions: he was trapped in an imaginary world. I stressed the need for medication to help him overcome this episode. Douglas then agreed to have the doctor come in, even though a doctor represented a threatening figure who could label him 'crazy'.

While he was talking to the doctor, I started to vibrate again. As a psychologist, I have always sought to integrate behavioural and psychological aspects with the spiritist doctrine. Moreover, several studies point out that stress is the field of medicine that combines body and soul. Therefore, it is intimately linked to spirituality, from my point of view.

Following the spiritual lessons detailed by André Luiz/Francisco Cândido Xavier in the book 'No Mundo Maior'[17], written in 1947, our brain has three distinct areas: the initial one, where automatism is found, which is in the subconscious plane; the motor cortex, that incorporates today's conquests and is in the conscious area; and that of the frontal lobes, representing the superior ideal and objective, and which are linked to the superconscious. The balance between these three areas leads us to the balance and development of our human side, which consequently leads to spiritual growth.

When I returned to the room, I could feel him calmer, so we urged him to allow the medicine to be administered. Douglas then called me a traitor and said I had allied myself with those who wanted to persecute him. I asserted that I only sought to do what was best for that moment. Finally, after several more negotiations, he gave his permission.

An injection was given, and Douglas left the room, resigned to his predicament. *What I believe*

The cure for any problem, including emotional illnesses, is within us and can be achieved by comprehending our life story.

This journal reflects the resilience and the search to settle down the flow of emotions that impregnate our day-to-day life. In other words, it shows that overcoming our afflictions is possible, and we can have a brilliant life.

---

17. TN – 'In the greater world' can be found on Amazon as part of the 'Life in the spirit world' Collection.

Acknowledgements

My everlasting girlfriend, wife and companion Aline Gonzaga Moreira and our sons, Guilherme and Ricardo

My mother, Deise Esteves, Abilio Rodrigues Braga (in memoriam) and my sister Glaucia Gonçalves

My father, Edison Gonçalves (in memoriam), and my stepmother Miriam Gonçalves

My uncle Eliseu Paulo Gonçalves and aunt Eugenia do Carmo Gonçalves

My parental figures, Maria Alice Peres Lisboa (in memoriam) and Eng. Roberto Medeiros Lisboa (in memoriam)

My paternal grandparents, Avelino Gonçalves (in memoriam) and Odete Gonçalves (in memoriam)

My maternal grandparents, Guilhermino Esteves (in memoriam) and Semíramis Petri Esteves (in memoriam)

My parents-in-law, Luiz Carlos Moreira and Lucia Gonzaga Moreira

My sister-in-law Dr. Flavia Moreira Miguel and her husband, Dr. Roberto Pereira Miguel

My cousins José Eduardo Lopes, Maria Lucia Olivieri, Miriam Moreira da Costa, Paulo Ferraz, Rodrigo Stoppa, Simone Giudice and Sylas Esteves Jeronymo

My friends: Alê Prade, Carlos Alberto Almeida, Cris Ferraz Prade, Cristina Braga, Frank Pruvost, Heloisa Pizzato Fialho, Jacinta Pereira, Dr. Marcelo Occhiutto, Marco Hennies, Mauricio Matteucci Reis, Ricardo Ferreira Xavier, Roberto Sollberger Jeolas and Trevor Wratten

And Bailey Moreira, our red labradoodle, born in Caerphilly, Wales: a faithful friend for all seasons.

About the Author

Douglas Gonçalves, 54 years old, from São Paulo, is married to Aline Gonzaga Moreira and is a father of 2 children, Guilherme and Ricardo. He is a hotelier with an MBA from LSE (London School of Economics). Gonçalves has worked for over 30 years in the area, in Brazil and overseas, in several countries, such as Mexico and England, and currently in Wales, United Kingdom, where he lives with his family.

Based on his life story, this journal brings a moving and reliable account that begins when the author had a psychotic breakdown in 2004, which made him a spectator of his own fate. He had to face the momentary loss of his faculties, a circumstance that severely affected his psychic functions and social relationships, marking his life forever.

His testimony provokes reflections on the current causes that triggered the breakdown, in an attempt to demystify the subject: according to medical statistics, one in four people will have mental health problems throughout their lives. It can also be a warning to those more susceptible to developing the disease, helping their families identify it quickly. Additionally, doctors can understand more aspects of such a crisis with Gonçalves' testimony, since it is an unusual experience considering that most patients do not remember anything.

Last but not least, the author decided to report his psychotic breakdown episode so that people suffering from mental struggles know they are not alone. In the same way, the journal can be a reference for a more patient-centred treatment to help in the healing process: in Gonçalves' case, a significant association with his ancestry. All in all, the book tells the search for understanding the most profound psychological causes, the importance of habit changes and spiritual re-education as prophylactic effects, and what is most surprising and significant: everything from the patient's perspective!

A portion of the proceeds will be donated to the non-governmental organisation Espaço Ser.

Who we are

We are an ecumenical NGO run by volunteers, not for profit, and maintained through donations. We are located in the Westside of São Paulo, with IN-PERSON and ONLINE services. Therefore, we can help people from all over the world, provided that they speak Portuguese.

We offer Complementary Practices (based on the Ottawa Charter – WHO) as a complementary treatment to psychological and psychiatric ones.

We assist people in emotional distress or with personality disorders, major depression, chronic anxiety or any syndrome with self-destructive symptoms or suicidal ideation.

https://www.espacoser.org.br/site

Printed in Great Britain
by Amazon

21713691R00061